Still

God ^ Loves To Do the Impossible.

Through You.

THE PRAYER OF ASA©
IN ACTION

W. Neil Gallagher, Ph.D.

King Asa

The Prayer of Asa

```
************************************************
```

"Listen to my friend Dr. Gallagher on the radio… and read his book."-

Zig Ziglar

Dr. Gallagher & Dr. Stanley at Praise Fest

```
************************************************
```

"I recommend you read Dr. Gallagher's 'The Prayer of Asa' because when we fight our battles on our knees, we win every time."

'Asa' Excerpts

Max Lucado must have been crushing jungle brush and stomping black scorpions right behind me as we entered Hoey Kee, "Village of Waste"... the home of lepers... Max got the description right when he said...

—from 1A – "Living With Lepers"

* * * * * * * * *

If you're reading this book, it's because the publishers know it has IMPACT:

THE TEXAS HOUSE PROPOSED A BILL TO DENY GRANDPARENTS ACCESS TO GRANDCHILDREN. Bill 2084.

The consequences of this bill to families in Texas— and throughout America— are as wild and deadly as swine flu. The Prayer of Asa smashed this bill and stopped the spread of this emotional plague that would have killed many innocent families... families who need the love, wisdom, and support of grandparents.

That's impact!

—from 1C – "The Impossible Adoption: Two of Them!"

* * * * * * * * *

They didn't tell me the mafia would wire-bomb my car when we shoved porn off the shelves and locked the adult stores. But the warning came; I ignored it, and then—

—from 1F – "Ambush on ABC"

"No one should fear to undertake any task in the name of our savior if it is just and if the intention is purely for His holy service."

—Christopher Columbus
From his journals and just before launching
a divinely-appointed task to eventually
discover the Americas.

"Every good achievement is created and energized by God."

—Max Lucado, *He Still Moves Stones*

Are you ready:

- For your life to be a miracle of God's power and service?
- To ask God to flow through you with every act, with every word? Join Dr. Gallagher in enjoying the power of a small prayer overcoming big obstacles. You'll see how one small prayer turns mediocrity into miracles, ruin into victory, depression into triumph, and doubt into ecstasy. You'll see how one forty-word prayer anoints you with God's purpose and pleasure. With *The Prayer of Asa,* you'll exult daily in the divine joy you were born to celebrate.

The Asa Prayer

> LORD, there is no one like You
>   to help the powerless against the mighty.
> Help us, LORD our God,
>   for we rely on You,
> and in Your Name
>   we have come against this vast army.
> LORD, You are our God;
>   do not let mere mortals
> prevail against You.

> —2 Chronicles 14:11 TNIV

Forty-eight words of passion, power, praise, and victory. Waiting for you. Are you ready?

Asa and You

Asa smacked Cush and crashed chariots.

Bad idea.

Cush was

bigger

…badder

…meaner

The swat team of the ancient world,
A blitzkrieg of barbarians who would have made the
Holocaust look like a pillow fight.

Cush had 1,000,000 men and thousands of chariots. Asa
had half that.

Las Vegas odds: 2 to 1. And the house always wins. Right?

"Asa's gonna' get crushed."

But he didn't. He conquered.

He voiced a prayer that has come cascading through the
centuries to empower God's man and God's woman to conquer
the impossible.

What's *your* million-man army, your impossible challenge?

I'll tell you mine. Then we'll look at the impossible challenges faced by prayer warriors like George Mueller, Protector
of Orphans; Dr. Kenneth Cooper, Father of Preventive
Medicine; S. Truett Cathy, Founder of Chick-fil-A restaurants; and Dave Ramsey, master of the TOTAL MONEY
MAKEOVER and mentor to millions on money management.

Then we'll look at *your* impossible challenges.

And you'll see that Asa is alive and well.

For you.

Right now.

CONTENTS

．

Photos & Credits

- Zig Ziglar's endorsement, Introduction
- Charles Stanley endorsement, Introduction
- Peace Corps Certificate – William N. Gallagher, p. 5
- Hut in Mae Hong Son at the confluence of Burma and Thailand, p. 6
- How to Stop the Porno Plague book cover, p. 84
- Joel Osteen and Dr. W. Neil Gallagher, p. 106
- Dr. Kenneth Cooper and wife Millie, Dr. W. Neil Gallagher, p. 112
- Mike Huckabee and Dr. W. Neil Gallagher, p. 115
- Truett Cathy, Dr. W. Neil Gallagher, and Scotty Gallagher, p. 119
- Warren Buffett letter, p. 120
- Gail Gallagher with son Matthew Nikilesh, p. 34
- Gail, Matthew Nikilesh, and W. Neil Gallagher, p. 37
- Author Gail Gallagher, p. 39

ISBN: 978-1-48356-384-8 (Print)

ISBN: 978-1-48356-385-5 (eBook)

Chapter 1

Asa in Action

1A- Living with Lepers
อาศัยอยู่กับขี้เรื้อน

"Ask not what your country can do for you,
but what you can do for your country."

President John F. Kennedy

Good quote from my hero at that time, JFK.

Here's a better quote:

"Ask not what you can possibly do for God,
but how God will do the IMPOSSIBLE through you."

Dr. W. Neil Gallagher

UNITED STATES OF AMERICA

PEACE CORPS

Hereby commends

𝖂illiam 𝔑.𝔊allagher

for dedication to her country and service to the people of

𝔗hailand

as a Peace Corps Volunteer

from June 17, 1963   to May 15, 1965

Sargent Shriver

My hut in Mae Hong Son at the confluence of Burma and Thailand

1A - Living with Lepers
อาศัยอยู่กับขี้เรื้อน

Don't look for it, because it's not there.

Teak sliced. Vines ripped. Beasts ran.

The Mae Hong Son of today sports more green than Chiang Mai's concrete, and it's cooler than Bangkok's fire, but the jungle primeval of Mae Hong Son, my village home 50 years ago, is gone.

Vanished.

Melted to the heat of progress.

Tribesmen in this Thai/Burmese[⊠] mountain range still harvest poppy, dictated by warlords, now driven deeper into the lush tangle of bush and mountain.

But don't look for my jungle hut among them. It's not there, gone forever. Fifty years ago when this saga unfolded, my corner of this Thai-Burmese jungle was thick with teak tribesmen, their sweaty knees locked around the massive ears of elephants as they hauled teak to rushing mountain streams. Fifty years ago, this jungle was home to tigers, cobras, and water buffaloes as wild and widespread as buffaloes on the American plains a century ago.

Back then, Thai workers didn't want assignments here in this lost corner of Northwest Thailand. No roads, phones, electricity, entertainment, or running water. To the government clerk, teacher, or sweat laborer assigned here for a mandatory two years of service, it meant banishment. The boonies. The Siberia of Thailand.

Today, it's the Aspen of Southeast Asia. Parades of bikes have replaced the parades of elephants, and packs of tourists have replaced the prides of tigers. Where scorpions the size of baby lobsters once darted across jungle paths, tourists now shuffle on flat paths in open-toed sandals. Hikers now carry cameras and sunglasses rather than machetes and daggers.

The cool, clean air of today's Mae Hong Son provides relief from the hot choking fumes of Chiang Mai and Bangkok. Mae Hong Son now has roads and an airport. The Mae Hong Son of my pre-med Peace Corps days is gone, like the quiet seaport settings of Riverhead, New York, are gone (lamented by New Yorkers), or a bucolic fishing village called Santa Barbara, California, gone (lamented by Californians). Ol' Timers cry for the old days of pristine beauty, dazzling sunsets, pure air, and wildlife playgrounds.

Gone.

* * *

Chiang Mai and Bangkok… might as well have been New York or California. Felt like I was a million miles from civilization that Saturday morning hunkered at the cold stream—a tributary of the Salween—beating clothes on rocks next to Pranee and friends.

Five-thirty that morning, I was up and built my small fire. I boiled my water to make warm tea, washing down my breakfast of rice and shredded coconut. I dumped my shirts, underwear, and socks in a basket and tied my pakama around my waist.

Love my loyal, durable, flexible pakama: that long purple-yellow-gray rectangular cloth, twice the size of a beach towel. Having the pattern of a checkerboard, it unfurled to be whatever you-wanted-it-to-be:

- towel,
- belt,
- turban,
- kerchief,
- blanket,
- tourniquet,
- club,
- bandage,
- even a roof for a lean-to shelter.

I fanned my pakama out in back of me to its full length, pulled the ends forward, and wrapped it around my waist. Its tail brushed the front of my knees and dropped to the ground. I bent forward, took the tail, twisted it, and shoved it up under my groin, connecting the tail of the pakama to the small of my back and stuffing it in hard and tight against my tailbone.

An adult diaper.

Now I can squat modestly and comfortably when I get to the stream.

I flip-flopped to the stream in back of my hut. I lifted a shirt from my bundle, plunged it into the cold water with a bar of hard soap, the size of a matchbox. I scrubbed, banged, and rinsed along with Pranee and friends who are hunkering around the stream.

สวัสดี ครับ คุณปราณี สบายดีหรือเปล่า.

"Good morning, Pranee. How are you," I say.

สบายดี. ขอบคุณค่ะ.

"Fine, thank you."

คุณรู้จัก ห้วยกี ไหมครับ

"Are you familiar with Hoey Kee?"

รู้จัก นิดหน่อยค่ะ.

คุณรู้จักทางที่จะไปที่นั่นไหมครับ.

"Do you know how I get there?"

ไม่แน่ใจก: อยู่ในป่าสักที่สูงๆข้าง อยู่ใกล้กับพม่า

"Not really. High in the teak jungle. Listen for the elephants, near Burma."

เคยมีใครไปที่นั่นบ้างไหมล่ะ ?

"Does anyone ever go there?"

เท่าที่ฉันทราบมา ใครที่ไปที่นั่นแล้ว ไม่เคยกลับมาอีกเลยก:

"All I know… people go there and never come back."

Never come back. Never come back. Never come back.

Is THAT where Nakon is? My mind races to last Thursday's assembly at the mountain school where I am a Peace Corps teacher. We stood as usual that Thursday morning shivering in the mountain fog hanging over us. Fifty-five degrees does not feel cold unless all you're wearing is a short-sleeved shirt and jungle shorts.

When is the sun going to burn through and thaw us out?

Same thought every morning.

Same wait for warmth: one-and-a-half hours.

I stood in back, erect, with the other teachers.

I was the only *farang* in the group.

This was the assignment I requested: a distant mountain village. I wanted to live, speak, and eat like a Thai.

A village Thai.

I shivered.

And I watched the students shiver as the headmaster finished his announcements. We stood erect for the Thai national anthem.

ประเทศไทยรวมเลือดเนื้อชาติเชื้อไทย
เป็นประชารัฐ ไผทของไทยทุกส่วน
อยู่ดำรงคงไว้ได้ทั้งมวล
ด้วยไทยล้วนหมาย รักสามัคคี
ไทยนี้รักสงบ แต่ถึงรบไม่ขลาด
เอกราชจะไม่ให้ใครข่มขี่
สละเลือดทุกหยาดเป็นชาติพลี
เถลิงประเทศชาติไทยทวี มีชัย ชโย

We finished with the stirring phrase: "Thais will serve their country with pride and prestige full of victory. Chai Yo (Cheers)."

As students marched from the flagpole toward the no-window and no-doors school building at the base of the mountain that looked more like an open log cabin of the early West, I asked one of my students, "Asaneenia, has Nakon been sick? I haven't seen him for a week."

"No, Uachai Santeepap. (My Thai name: Man of Peace.) They took him to live with his parents at Hoey Kee."

"Hoey Kee? Where and what is that?"

I asked teachers and students throughout the day; I learned that it's a leper colony. And it means "Village of Waste," they say.

"Can't be," I protest.

I know the word for "village" is mòo bâhn. Where does the "Kee" come from? And "waste or toilet"? The word is hôrng náhm.

How do they get *Hoey Kee* out of this? No one knew.

What they did know was: At the first sign of leprosy in this chungwat[1], that's where you're shipped, no questions asked. Everybody in the household goes.

Then what happens? Nobody knew that either.

That afternoon, I asked the chungwat health officer… He didn't know the answer.

"Well, when they're cured, if they're ever cured, do they ever come back to live a normal life?"

---

1 Province.

"I don't know that, either."

Can't be. Can't be.

Those Hollywood scenes from *Ben Hur*... Charlton Heston (Ben Hur) discovers his sister and mother dumped in leprosy caves on the edge of Jerusalem. Hollywood shows them with flour-white complexions, purplish-black splotches on their faces erupting like blackberries. They're dumped in leprosy caves, deep and dark, banished and forgotten.

Surely these gentle, caring people, the Thais whom I've grown to love so much would not just abandon friends and family to that kind of a terminal, painful, and disgusting fate.

I'm going to see for myself.

Come Saturday, and I will abandon my washing chores and go there.

I'll hike to Hoey Kee. Best information I get is that it's 14 miles from Mae Hong Son, somewhere off the jungle path that leads to Burma and somewhere near the headwaters of the Salween, pressing against the Thai-Burmese Mountains.

* * *

Five a.m. Saturday, I fill my canteen with boiled water. I lay out my pakama and place in its middle eight kernels of kanoon and four kluag maj (miniature bananas). I wrap the upper and lower folds of my pakama around my self-made backpack, grab the two ends of the pakama, one with my right hand, one with my left, stretch it out, and twist it, so that the centerpiece pouch now is a tight container for my lunch. I tie the pakama around my waist with the kanoon and kluag maj tight against the small of my back.

I smear legs, arms, face, ears, and neck with the rancid, government-issued repellent from my Peace Corps kit. I then slap on top of it creamy sunblock, its white lotion a protection against sun and its coconut fragrance a protection against the repellant stench. I shove my Boston Red Sox cap tightly around my skull, don fresh white socks, and stuff my feet into high-topped sneakers. I march down the muddy path out of Mae Hong Son due west...

toward the mountains...

through the jungle…

to Hoey Kee.

I start at sunup, so I'll be back by sundown… assuming I find Hoey Kee at all.

Pranee was right on: About seven miles, I see the snake-thin path to my right… another seven or eight miles to Hoey Kee, I guess. The path leads to the river. Go to the river,

follow the river,

follow the river,

follow the river,

I was told.

I follow the path along the river, placing one foot in front of the other like I'm walking on top of a balancing beam.

Man… shoulda' worn my jeans.

Thorns slash my legs, attracting dime-sized mosquitoes and nickel-sized leeches to feast on my open, bleeding scratches. The fragrant lotion apparently smothered the repellant and has become white frosting for my hungry attackers. I slide the towel from around my neck and tie its ends to make a big knot, a white club to smash this army of blood-sucking cannibals feasting on my legs.

The further I get from Mae Hong Son, the more I see piles of dung. Not big enough for elephant patty. Thicker and wider than dog patty. I hear the bellows and see a row of black, curved horns.

I hear a crash and see to my left a massive water buffalo, its head stiff and erect, pointed toward me, its nostrils round, wide, and wet like the bottom of two beer bottles. She stops, sniffs, snorts, and turns away… satisfied I'm not a threat to her calf.

A family of monkeys screams at my intrusion. A scorpion larger than my foot darts in front of me.

I ignite my pace to a sprint, still balancing in the thin path. I run a mile, maybe two. And I hear a symphony. It's the euphonic sound of rushing water, gurgling, churning, cascading over rocks.

I run to the sound, and I see four huts hugging the river. This is Huey Blah, the first village that Pranee told me I would see, Village of Fish. Each hut is the size of a Boy Scout tent, perched high above the ground with four sticks holding it aloft, one in each corner of the house, each stick no wider than the shaft of a broom.

I walk toward the huts, and I freeze.

To my right, about half the length of a basketball court away, I see an ornate… well… an ornate dollhouse on stilts. Too big for a birdhouse. What is it? Who's housing miniature dolls? I shuffle closer, and I see that it sports an orange-shingled roof, festooned with green trinkets around its sides and a swirling, flaming red turret at the top, stretching toward the sky. What is it…?

I feel a cape of darkness dropping over me as I approach this house of mystery. I feel a chill against my cheeks, and I feel small hairs standing on the back of my neck.

Wha…? Wha…? It's the Pĕa. The spirits. The wild, demonic, and unknown spirits of the Pĕa who must be placated every day. Our cultural study in Buddhism, part of our Peace Corps training, told us about the prevalence of Pĕa in this Buddhist culture, notably in the distant villages and jungle areas.

I shuffle closer, my curiosity drawing me to a tray, more like a toy canoe, in front of the tiny door of the Pĕa house. The tray holds chunks of bananas and crumbs of coconut. Lizards dart away, and a menacing gecko stays glued to the top of the roof, tongue flashing.

These villagers (Yes, I remember reading about this in our cultural studies.) —they're feeding the Pĕa every day, placating these unseen forces, the Pĕa. These are the demonic spirits who control their lives.

That's it! That's the reason, if there is a Hoey Kee and people are banished out here somewhere, that's the reason nothing is done. Their lives are controlled by demons which they think no one can control.

I stare at the gecko.

Surely these villagers know it's not Pĕa eating their morning offering of bananas or coconuts. It's the lizards and the monkeys.

WHAT A DIFFERENCE CHRIST MAKES!!

What a BIG difference our God makes, the God of the Bible. This is real. This is it. We know a God of love and power and caring, not a god that has to be placated with scraps of food. No vague, arbitrary, or fearful sprinkling of appeasement for an unknown god.

Words from Isaiah hit me: "How lost they are who pray to gods who cannot save... There is no God apart from me, a righteous God and a Savior." (Isaiah 45: 20, 21)

And, it races through my mind, the truth of Isaiah 2:8:

> Their land is full of idols; they bow down to the work of
> their hands, to what their fingers have made.
>
> —Isaiah 2:8 NIV

My hypnotic and chilling fascination staring into this denizen of demons is interrupted by the whack, whack, whack of a mallet. I turn to my left to see, outside the nearest hut, a woman whacking hulls of rice with a wooden mallet—same way these villagers have crushed rice for centuries. I walk to her, and a young boy runs to me. He's six or seven years old. Large, almond-shaped eyes, caramel-brown. He approaches, boasting a thin, cautious, and widening smile.

"Uachai?"

He knows my name.

I later found out that my "fame" as the only farang in Mae Hong Son has preceded me in this changwat, even to its distant villages.

He takes me to his mother. I reach back to my pakama and take out two bananas and two large kernels of kan⊠on, give them to the boy and his mother, and they devour them as gleefully as though they'd never had fruit. I ask about Hoey Kee.

They point. "Follow the river. Follow the river. Follow the river. Do you have a gun or a knife? You might see opium bandits coming down from the hills. We haven't seen a tiger for a long time," they assure me. "Just follow the river. Watch for the yellow cobra. Keep your big knife in your hand."

Now there is no path. I hack my way with my machete, following the river northwest.

Surely, no one else comes out here. How do they get food?

15

As I stomp through the high brush, I see that the pores dotting my legs are thin faucets of blood streaming into my high-top sneakers. I feel the red liquid squishing underneath my heels. I slide my towel again from my neck and whack at a new army of mosquitoes and leeches. I wipe away pools of blood forming at the top of my socks.

I'm going back. If Hoey Kee is here, someone else will have to bring me to it. In a boat. Or on top of an elephant. Or someone else is going to have to locate these people and find out what's going on.

A clearing, and I see it. It's the size of the inside of a baseball diamond. Around the clearing are 11 huts, frail and thin, like the ones I'd seen in Huey Blah. The one to my right, where first base would be, has got to be the hut of the headmaster. Headmaster is always the first hut. Thai courtesy requires you to go to the headmaster first.

Max Lucado must have been in back of me as I approached the bamboo porch of this first leper: *"He stoops like a hunchback. His fingerless hand, draped in rags, extends toward you, pleading. A tattered wrap hides his face except for two pain-filled eyes."*[2]

This figure, barely visible in the back of the hut, is squatted on a stretch of bamboo sheets. He squats like a chimpanzee. I can see that his arms flow into stumps like the end of a baseball bat. He shuffles to the front of the hut, and he lifts his stumps into a prayerful-like gesture, a waj. I clasp my hands into the same gesture and bow toward him. I stumble as I say, "Sawadee, Khrub. Sabaj-Dee. Ry?" ("Hello, sir, how are you?")

I stutter my greeting, because I feel hypocritical asking how he is. His face is round and smooth like a volleyball. His eyes have recessed into his skull. There are no ears. For a nose, there are two button-size holes underneath his eyes. I continue. "Uachai. Man of Peace. I'm a teacher from Mae Hong Son. My name is Uachai."

He says, "Gwallel." ("How are you," in Khan dialect.)

I answer, "Gualair." ("I'm okay," Khan dialect.) I then ask, "Khun poot Thai dai mai?" ("Do you speak Thai?")

"Chai. (Yes,)" he assures me.

His eyes have a gauzy film over them, like he's looking at me through

2 Max Lucado, *He Still Moves Stones* (Nashville: Thomas Nelson, 1999) 4.

a fishbowl. As he speaks, I see there are no teeth. He attempts to smile as he tells me his story. He tells me how leprosy attacks and destroys. And alienates.

His name is Tonkchan. He was a clerk in another village, Maesaering, in this changwat. When the locals determined that he had leprosy, he was shipped off to Hoey Kee with his wife.

His wife has died.

He tells me he's been here 11 years. He continues his narrative about the creeping progression of leprosy: it slowly destroys the nerve endings. That's why his toes have worn away and his ears have worn away, no stimulation at the extremities. Skin, then flesh, wears out and flakes off. Ears, fingers, toes. He tells me that by sheer endurance, he is now the oldest one in Hoey Kee and is recognized as the Ajan, the headmaster.

"I look and smell bad, I know. You can stay away if you want."

"Can I bathe you, wash you, get you clean clothes?"I ask.

"We're afraid when we take off our clothes. Peels away skin. We cannot bathe… the water rubs off more skin.

"I am almost blind. It's because of the dust and insects in my eyes. I cannot blink. Two people in government uniforms come by once a month and drop ten sacks of rice on the riverbank. They don't get out of their boat. I have seen them. They throw the sacks of rice and scream, Bpai! Bpai![3]. Then they shoot down the river like water spiders on top of water."

Ten bags of rice and whatever fruit they can pluck and monkeys they can roast. That's it.

I sit sideways on his bamboo floor, my feet in back of me, a sign of respect for my elder. I feel tears pooling at the corner of my eyes, and I feel their wet salt trickling over my cheekbones. I ask if he can tell me more about these families in Hoey Kee.

And I ask, "Hoey Kee? Where does that name come from?"

He says, "ห้องน้ำ , หมู่บ้านชาวเขา.

Hôrng náhm, mòo bâh chao kăo… toilet, or waste, and hill tribe village… Waste Village. That's how they've compressed it in the Northern dialect: Waste Village or Hoey Kee, Village of Waste.

3 The English equivalent: "Let's get the hell out of here!"

We slide off the bamboo matting to the hot, dusty ground. He squats beside me and shuffles like a monkey on a leash. We walk around this inner diamond, taking a tour of the other huts in the positions where second base, shortstop, and third base would be. Stunned faces stare out at me like creatures on exhibit. They're curious, and scared. Slowly, they slide from their huts, and each man and woman raises his or her hands in a waj, then break into crooked smiles.

I see that their clothes are also stuck on their bodies. But none of them are as decayed as Tonkhan, my new friend. A family in their 30s turns to the dark interior of their hut and shouts a command. A boy comes out. It's Nakon. Doesn't look to me like Nakon is infected. The parents clearly have decay, but to my naked eyes as a layman, it doesn't appear to me that Nakon is infected. Not at all.

I hunker in the middle of this diamond and beckon for every family to join me in a small circle. I empty my pakama, slice my remaining bananas and kanoon into quarters, and distribute what I have. I spend the rest of the afternoon here with them squatted in front of me in small circles. I ask each person his or her story.

After listening to 11 tales of woe and misery and despair, I rise to leave, and Nakon's father says to me, "Len tekrew maj." ("Do you play tekrew?)

"Chai, Khrub," I respond.

Nakon's father darts into the dark hut and runs out with a straw ball. Tekrew is a straw ball we use for "soccer in a circle," I call it.

I've played it many times with students at school.

Nakon's father gathers his son and the men to form a small circle. They take their ragged pakamas and wrap them around their feet. In tekrew, you bat this straw ball, the size of a softball, back and forth to each other across the circle. No hands allowed. You can use your shoulder, elbows, knee, ankle, foot, head... but no hands. Soccer in the air... except the goal is to keep the tekrew in the air as you bang it back and forth to each other across the circle.

They scream in glee. Haven't had this much fun in years.

I insist I have to leave. It'll take several hours to get back, and I'm not going to stomp down those paths in the dark. I promise I will return.

I march down my machete-hacked path rapidly. An hour and a half later, I pass by Huey Blah and then the house of Pêa. I find the thin trail that I'd created and crushed earlier. I jogged two and a half hours to return to the main trail. The sun's setting quickly now. I run, and I sweat, and my knees feel weak, and my joints ache. I arrive at my hut at dusk. Clothes on, I stumble to the cold stream and wash the sweat, the stings, the sores from my now-shaking body. I return to my hut, lay down with mosquito net draped over me.

And I burn.

I burn with anger that these people have been abandoned. How could this happen? I burn with fear. How am I going to help them? And I burn with fire, the fire that Jeremiah felt, fire in my bones. It's not right that any of God's people should suffer so much without help, without hope. I burn with the prayerful determination of Asa. I commit, with God's help, to find a rescue strategy somewhere, somehow.

This is a million-man army, and my resources are so small.

This is definitely not an exercise in self-help.

I continue to burn. Really burn. I take my temp. It's 106°, I'm shivering. Frozen slush flows under my skin and knocks my jaw into spasms. I chatter so loud I can hear my teeth whacking against each other, echoing off the walls of my hut. Fluids explode from my mouth. Fluids explode from my anus. I sit on the crude pot beside by bed for hours. My head pounds, and my body shakes. I wrap blankets around me to no avail. Violent diarrhea comes every five minutes. I crawl to the gray first-aid suitcase, my Peace Corps ER treasure. With the back of my hand, I shovel aside bottles of pills, ointments, splints, salve, Band-Aids, looking for antibiotics.

Antibiotics?

Yes, they put antibiotics in here! Thank God! With a trembling hand, I grab a small flashlight, also in the first-aid kit, and read the tiny print: "Take only under direction of a medical professional or when there is life-threatening event. Take two and wait two hours." I take four and collapse. I burn and puke and defecate for six more hours. I lose track of time.

I awake, and I'm sweating. The steaming tropical sun seeps through spaces in my leaf roof. I'm hot now. It's 1:00 p.m. on Sunday. The chills have stopped. My temperature's 99°. No diarrhea. My canteen water is warm and stale, but it tastes cool and delicious.

I crawl to the hut of Suchai, the math teacher in our village school, urging him to please send his son to get the chungwat nurse. When the nurse returns, I tell her my story. With a quick examination, she tells me she does not think this is leprosy or the early signs of it. Leprosy does not have these violent symptoms. She tells me that I have been attacked by amoebic dysentery and maybe a touch of malaria. She asks me when the last time was I took my Aralin.

I can't remember. She assures me I can take two more antibiotics. She removes them from the first-aid kit and helps me swallow them with two gulps of the warm canteen water.

Suchai and his family prepare warm tea for me and cook a gruel made from rice and sugar.

I sleep the rest of Sunday, and I awake at 6:00 a.m. Monday. I eat slivers of papaya, munching on them slowly, and sip a cup of coconut juice.

On Monday I'm well enough to return to school. After school, I meet with, and plead with, the chungwat health officer. "Nothing we can do about it. Controlled by Bangkok. Our orders: 'stay away.'"

God, make my life a miracle of your service. You brought me here for a reason. This looks like it's impossible. But YOU DO THE IMPOSSIBLE through people like me who feel weak and overwhelmed.

God responded to Asa back then, I reasoned, and that same God is still around.

I returned to Hoey Kee the following Saturday,
> and the following,
>> and the following.

Each week, I stuffed my pakama with bananas, bandages, ointment, and aspirin.

I have hands-on medical skills. Worked my way through college as a hospital aide in a small hospital on the outskirts of Boston.

Told the medical staff I was Pre-Med, and they swiftly and gladly interned me to perform procedures that, today, only a doctor or R.N. would perform. On those long weekend shifts, I…

- spoon-fed the sick,
- inserted catheters,
- stuck IVs in the arms of recovery-room patients,
- gave shots,
- scrubbed with surgeons,
- comforted the dying,
- helped with autopsies, and
- slapped paddles on patients to jerk them back to life.

Training came in handy.

With limited knowledge and limited supplies, I hiked to Hoey Kee Saturday after Saturday to give hope, relief, and encouragement. I gave them my clothes except, literally, what I had on my back. I learned that by applying Vaseline to their tortured skin, I could gradually peel away old cloth and give them a gentle sponge bath. By the way, if you're ever wandering in the mountains of Northern Thailand and see people wearing caps, jackets, or sweaters that say Kappa Delta Phi or caps and t-shirts that say Red Sox, you know where they got them.

I wrote to the Women's Club, American Embassy in Bangkok. Via special plane, they sent bulging boxes of shirts, jackets, trousers, blankets, sandals, socks, and more medical supplies.

God bless them.

I felt like a parched man on a desert island opening those cartons as though they were jugs of cool water. I cried and I laughed. The boxes appeared monthly. The planes landed on our ersatz airstrip, the far end of a dry rice patty.

Fellow teachers helped me haul the boxes to the back of elephants. The hill tribesmen on their well-trained pacaderms pressed through the jungle paths with me to deliver the supplies.

I wrote the head of the Peace Corps in Thailand, John McCarthy, and begged him to come up and visit Hoey Kee. He did. We then tactfully went to Thai health officials and asked if more could be done. They said *yes*.

I received permission to take Nakon to McKean Leprosy Hospital in Chiang Mae. In my study of leprosy and, asking more questions, I had learned about McKean: a Christian school, hospital, and sanitarium for lepers, founded by Presbyterian missionaries in 1908.

I learned that Nakon did not have leprosy. I received permission from his parents to have him return to live with relatives in Mae Hong Son, allowing him to have a normal, family-related, healthy life, and be available to see his parents on occasional visits. Everyone loved that solution.

Months now rolled into years, and my time of assignment was up. Local officials, along with Peace Corps officials, agreed to follow up on the visits. By the time I left Mae Hong Son, food, medicine, and helpers were going to Hoey Kee weekly.

Lepers were NOT the untouchables screamed at and shunned in many cultures. It's not impossible to touch… teach… heal… and love them.

God loves to do the impossible, and that divine passion is not thwarted by mountains, jungle, or disease.

Why… with the prayer of Asa… you can even take on the million-man army of Tye Beecher.

* * * * * * * *

1B - Homeless to Homecoming

1B – Homeless to Homecoming

One more time.
One more time, Neil.
Can I do this one more time?
I hear the moaning,
        whining,
                pleading.
…followed by the rap
              rap
                      rapping
and the tap
              tap
                  tapping
at my Boston door.
    February. Five degrees.
    Like Poe:

        Once upon a midnight dreary, while I pondered,
        weak and weary,
        Over many a quaint and curious volume of forgot-
        ten lore—
        While I nodded, nearly napping, suddenly there
        came a tapping,
        As of some one gently rapping, rapping at my cham-
        ber door.
        "'Tis some visitor," I muttered, "tapping at my cham-
        ber door:
            Only this, and nothing more."

Ah, distinctly I remember, it was in the
bleak December,
And each separate dying ember wrought its ghost
upon the floor.

Could it be? Yes, it is. The ghost at my door is real and stinks.
My nose recoils at the familiar odor of Tye. Right through the door it
flowed... the knock-you-down stench of whiskey and rotting garbage. Tye's
pleading for help. And I'm pleading for answers. Again.

I breathe the Asa prayer again:

> LORD, there is no one like You
>> to help the powerless against the mighty.
> Help us, Lord our God,
>> for we rely on You,
> and in Your Name
>> we have come against this vast army.
> Lord, You are our God;
>> do not let mere mortals
> prevail against You.

You are bigger than Tye and his problems.

What's God going to do with you, Tye? What am *I* going to do with
you? This is a million-man army, God, I pleaded, and I need your help
because I don't know what to do.

It began months earlier. Riding from library to home on the subway
that 5° day, I saw him, under a seat, rolled in a ball... stiff, hard, and moaning. I woke him and heard his tale of pain. I took him home to clean him
up from the inside out.

Like the Salvation Army motto: Soup, soap, salvation.

Wouldn't be the first time I scooped the homeless or desperate off the
street. My infinitely compassionate wife was used to it. Clear to me then and

clear to me now that, as a welfare waif in my youth, I knew that throwing money at poverty was not the answer.

Years earlier, I had placed a notice in the Yellow Pages under our church's name: "We're here to help. Call us. 24-hour number: _____."

And they called. And they came.

They ate at our table. They slept in our beds. They came to church with us.

Sonya, a beaten, depressed lesbian, face pock-marked like the surface of the moon, seeking escape from her dyke.

Tara, a beaten, depressed prostitute, welts on her back, seeking escape from her pimp.

We fed them, loved them, and by the grace of God, revived them.

I had written articles in *World Vision* pleading for every reader to aggressively reach out to the lost and desperate, pleading with every family to adopt a welfare or homeless family. This, I urged, was a practical and compassionate solution to poverty. And powerful enough to eliminate poverty in America within a year. This solution—called tough love—combined food and shelter with life skills training.

And renewal from the inside out. Billy Graham: "Jesus did not come to take people out of the slums but to take the slums out of people."

Starts on the inside… flows to the outside.

Uncomfortable solution, I admitted, this practice of hauling him home. But what else is new about the Christian life?

Francis Schaeffer in *The Mark of a Christian*: "Are you willing to let the unwanted and dirty into your home to vomit on your floor and soil your bed, and let them in again to love them and teach them and restore them? That is what L'Abri is about, and this is unconditional love. This is the mark of a Christian."

After talking to Tye that day and concluding that he wasn't shooting cocaine or carrying a gun, I called my wife and said I was bringing him home. She poured water in the beans and stuffed bread in the hamburger to stretch out the meatloaf. Tye came and slept on our couch and sat at our table with Gail and our kids.

Tye's story: good plumber, bad drinker. Each time he built his business, he'd guzzle again and give up again.

With God's help, on that icy afternoon, we were going to smash that destructive pattern and restore Tye to sobriety and significance. Took him home and cleaned him up. Sobered him up. Fattened him up. Got him a job. Gave him the Gospel and an opportunity to embrace it. Heard his confession of faith and baptized him. We restored his independence. Tye's on his own.

Weeks go by, and the call comes. "Neil, they don't like me at ABC Plumbing. I got mad and quit. I was feeling a little down after that, so I drank a little and lost the apartment."

We took him back, cleaned him up, and fed him. Clothes, apartment, job. Dignity again. AA counseling again. New job. Weeks fly, and the call comes. "Neil, they don't like me at that new place you sent me to… you know, Comet Plumbing."

Here we go: the pattern of the alcoholic. Accept no responsibility. Blame others.

Whiskey and collapse and gutter-living. Déjà vu.

We rescue him and restore him again. Health, hope, new job, and independence are his.

Three and a half weeks zip by, and it's now late December, and someone's tap-tap-tapping at my door.

"Neil, they didn't like me at Bay Plumbing. People there aren't very nice. I need help." The words flow over the door and spill into my reluctant ears.

What to say? What to do? My doctoral studies are suffering. My family is suffering. My energy and checkbook are draining. Worse, Tye is not responding. This is not easy.

"Sweet charity" may taste sweet to Tye, but it doesn't taste sweet to me.

Rick Warren's writings weren't around back then, but his recent blog summed it. "When times get tough and I get tired, I won't back up, back off, back down, back out, or backslide. I'll just keep moving forward by God's grace. I am mission focused, so I cannot be bought. I will not be compromised, and I shall not quit after I finish the race. To my Lord and Savior Jesus Christ, I say, 'However, whenever, wherever, whatever you ask me to do, the answer in advance is YES! Wherever you lead and whatever the cost, I am ready any time, any way."

A modern Asa.

I pray Asa, and I open the door. A blast of Arctic air slaps me in the face. I inhale and I feel an icy fist punch the back of my throat. I step outside and see holes in the crunchy snow where Tye has shuffled and stumbled up to the door. With arms folded, teeth chattering, and reeking of Night Train, Tye whines, "Neil, I needed to have a little shot to warm myself before I came." He repeats: "They don't like me at Bay Plumbing. Mean and hard. I had to quit and—"

"Stop!"

Tye raised his chin and looked at me with the droopy brown eyes of a hound dog fixed on his master waiting for the next command.

"After every meeting like this, Tye,"—I'm shivering faster than I'm lecturing—"after every one, I called the AA shelter. You told me each time you would go there and stay there until THEY said you were totally clean. Each time, you left early. That's it. You follow your snow tracks back down the path and go directly to the rescue shelter now. Get there in the same way you got here, and you stay there until they tell me you've sobered up. Then this home is open to you again and so is my family, my money, and my church. We'll help you with job, food… you know…"

"Neil, you've never been down there. They're just a bunch of do-gooders down th—"

"That's it, Tye. Go."

"Neil, please, please. Just for a week."

"No, Tye. Go. You probably won't understand what I'm saying. Maybe you'll never understand it, but I love you too much and God loves you too much to let this happen again. We love you enough to hold you responsible for your own behavior. Here's the deal, Tye. The folks at AA know you. You go to the AA shelter now. Open 24 hours. After they tell me you're sobered—for good—you can come back here and live with me. We'll find you a job, get you a place to live. We'll start all over again… We'll have a great big homecoming for you and—"

"Neil, if you don't help me, I'm going to the bridge."

THE BRIDGE… one of many spanning Boston Harbor, from which many had been pushed and others had jumped into the icy Atlantic.

I breathe a quick prayer for wisdom again.

And I heard these words explode. "Tye, if you do that, that's between you and God."

I closed the door, stunned at the origin and impact of my words.

* * * * * * * * *

Fast forward.

It's a bright and fresh May morning. New England sings with life. Brown ice-encrusted meadows have burst into lush green carpets. White birches stretch their arms to hug birds returning with their families. The mighty Atlantic is spotted with leisure craft swaying with the morning breezes, and its gray-green waters freeze the ankles of early and brave swimmers.

The phone rings. A clear, confident voice says, "Neil, how are you and your family?"

"We're doing fine. Who is this?"

"This is Tye. I'm in Hartford."

"Tye? Tye who?"

"Tye Beecher."

He unfolds the story. That December night was his turning point, he said. He DID go to AA. He DID stay, and he DID sober up. He then went to live with his daughter in Hartford, determined to make it this time. For good. He returned to church. He opened his own plumbing business. He called to thank me and God for holding . . . him . . . responsible.

That was a solution I could not have controlled or orchestrated. From Gallagher's perspective, it was impossible.

How did you do that? Why did you say that to him that night? How did you achieve that rescue?

And the answer is, I didn't. God did it. God gets the credit because He supplied the power to do the impossile.

Asa's alive and well. Domestically and internationally...

* * * * * * * * *

1C - The Impossible Adoption: Two of Them!

1C - The Impossible Adoption: Two of Them!

Wanna' know if it's nearly impossible to adopt internationally?

Ask Madonna:

USA TODAY: MADONNA RETURNS HOME EMPTY-HANDED: MALAWI JUDGE DENIES HER APPLICATION TO ADOPT GIRL[4]

Madonna has left Malawi.

On Sunday, two days after a judge in the African nation rejected her application to adopt 3 ½-year-old Mercy James, Madonna boarded a plane for London, the Associated Press reported. Judge Esme Chombo denied the singer's application Friday because of a residency requirement for prospective parents.

Will we have a roadblock like that in rescuing Matthew Nikilesh Gallagher? Nikilesh was his Indian name. We added the "Matthew" and the "Gallagher."

Way before Madonna, many attempts at international adoption had been crushed.

We feared our attempt would collapse, too.

Like Jacki and Mike Dudding's:[5]

Jacki and Mike Dudding began their adoption journey in February, when they attempted to adopt again from Guatemala.

---

4 Lorena Blas and Adrienne Thompson, "Madonna returns home empty-handed," *USA Today* April 6, 2009:2D.
5 Anna B. Tinsley, "With adopted Guatemalan girl finally home, 'This is where the new journey begins,'" *The Fort Worth Star-Telegram* 20 March 2008, Local News 1.

Then last March, Guatemalan officials froze pending cases to review facts and interview birth mothers because of concerns about fraud and illegal adoptions.

Their case was allowed to proceed only after a hold put on children at the private orphanage where Sienna lived—Semillas de Amor—was lifted by the government.

They visited Sienna several times in Guatemala, each time aching because they had to leave her behind. Mike went to Washington, D.C. to ask congressional and State Department adoption officials to help bring his daughter home.

And Jacki, with the help of Gladney, secured more than $16, 000 in donations for the orphanage, which had fallen behind on bills and risked being closed.

"This has been such an emotional roller coaster," said Jacki. "We would think we were almost at the end of the line, then they changed the rules. We're almost at the end again, and they lose a piece of paper. It keeps going on and on."

For our international mission, to rescue Nikilesh, we were told:

5) You'll have to go to India to live there six months.

6) You'll have to pay $10,000 to an attorney on the Indian side.

7) You'll have to pay $10,000 for an American lawyer to help.

8) You'll have to pay $10,000 to an international adoption agency to make arrangements. (They might as well have said $10 billion.)

9) And… there's still no assurance.

Each roadblock was a million-man army. Why bother?
Because we pledged it

- to God,
- to ourselves,
- and to needy children anywhere.

Gail Gallagher with their son Matthew Nikilesh.

Early in our marriage, Gail and I pledged: whatever number of biological children God blessed us with… that would be the number we would later adopt. We knew that there were billions of children who had no homes.

So… we had our two children and then went on a rescue mission. Few babies were available in America, since abortion was slaughtering infants like cattle in an abattoir. None left. We expanded our search overseas.

Gail found our Nikilesh in an orphanage shoved between shacks in a fetid alley in Bombay. The need was there, but "It'll never get done," we were told.

"Impossible," we were told. "For openers, no one from the States has ever adopted directly from India. Way too much bureaucracy."

"It's a useless and irrelevant effort," we were told. "Why bother? There are billions of starving babies in the world. What difference does it make?"

We reminded critics of the starfish story. Old man strolling the beach and, after low tide, grabs a starfish baking and rotting in the sun. He hurls the starfish back into the ocean, springing it into life again. A young surfer stops the old man and says, "What are you doing that for, mister? There are thousands spread out. Look down there. You can see them for miles. It doesn't make any difference." The old man grabbed another, hurling it into the cool ocean. And said, "Makes a difference to that one."

Made a difference to Nikilesh.

For Nikilesh, for ourselves, we prayed Asa:

> LORD, there is no one like You
>> to help the powerless against the mighty.
> Help us, LORD our God,
>> for we rely on You,
> and in Your Name
>> we have come against this vast army.
> LORD, You are our God;
>> do not let mere mortals
> prevail against You.

> Don't let mere mortals called
> bureaucrats stand against You and
> Your compassionate purposes.

This was in the 70s, long before the days of FedEx, texting, and the Internet. Best we had was snail mail, Western Union, and crackling phone calls made with the help of an overseas operator. Like a snail going uphill, months trudged by. Gail kept after it. She found that orphanage in Bombay, eager to help us and appreciative of our efforts.

Yes, a baby had just been deposited with them.

As the weeks crawled by, letters came to us on gauzy-thin rice paper. Legal documents flowed back and forth on long, soiled sheets held together at the top with string.

Nikilesh's story: His mother, begging on the street, had 13 children. She was not going to leave Nikilesh on the hot pavement to shrivel and die as thousands do. She loved him enough to find this orphanage and deposit him in safety.

Orphanage workers told us that when he was left at their step, he wasn't much bigger than a squirrel. That's why we've told him for the past 30 years, he's been twice blessed and twice loved… loved by a biological mother who loved him enough to find him shelter and loved enough to be sought after and adopted by us.

What a joy adoption is: *Twice loved. Loved by biological parents, loved by adoptive parents.* The bumper sticker is true: "Abortion is not the answer, adoption is."

Gail accelerated her calls and letters. Because of my studies and speaking responsibilities, Gail passionately did all the grunt work:

- A state inspector visited, gave us A+, and cheerfully supported our efforts.
- An Indian social worker visited and responded with equal enthusiasm.
- We found an Indian lawyer who took care of the details on the Indian side and charged us a grand total of $212.
- We found a domestic lawyer, also very supportive, who charged us a whopping $300 instead of $10,000.
- We found volunteer flight attendants, with Alaska Airlines, who delivered adopted children to homes in the U.S. God bless 'em!! Kisses and kudos.

So… eight months after we began our impossible efforts, we were handed Nikilesh at Theodore Green Airport. Not a dry eye at the airport. We rushed our fragile package home. We lay him in the middle of our king-sized bed, adorned with new and crisp white sheets, the gift wrapping for our Bombay blessing. Big brown eyes, snow-white teeth, and a rich chocolate glow. His tiny body sank in the middle of the bed like a Hershey's Kiss melting into marshmallow fluff.

Story's not over.

When Asa conquered his impossible army, the Bible says, he preserved a nation FOR THE FUTURE BENEFIT of millions. When we conquered this impossible army of cynicism and and discouragement, we unleashed a flood of blessings for the future benefit of many:

1) We were the first.

The *Providence Journal* discovered our impossible adoption and ran a front-page article seen by 900,000 people. My Gail—my God-loving, good-looking, good-cooking, beautiful blond, holding Matthew Nikilesh Gallagher. The front page!!

Gail, Matthew Nikilesh, and W. Neil Gallagher

"COUPLE ADOPT DIRECTLY FROM INDIA."

Calls came from Massachusetts, Rhode Island, and Connecticut from folks who had been trying to adopt internationally. We hosted a meeting. Twenty people came. From that, several more infants were rescued from orphanages in India.

And at Matthew's official adoption ceremony where he was awarded citizenship, the judge put into his tiny hands an American flag flown above the White House. Matthew still keeps that flag proudly displayed in his study.

The governor of Rhode Island invited us to his chambers for a photo shoot. More publicity. More opportunities to get the word out.

Gets better. Thirty years later, Matthew Nikilesh Gallagher, a Baylor grad and financial professional, has been awarded his CFP[6] license. He's married to a beautiful Christian woman and has received numerous "Outstanding Leadership" awards for his leadership and community services. He has grown into a strong Christian leader.

2) And Gail is now a counselor and writer on international adoptions, providing an urgently needed resource. Not only did she guide and counsel the couples mentioned above and help them secure their adoptions, but she has written for *International Adoptions Today* and *Christianity Today*. She's a staff writer for *Crosswalk*. Her vision and her motto is, "Simply never give up. These children need you. Claim to do the impossible and step out and do it."

---

6 Certified Financial Planner.

Gail Gallagher is a freelance writer, having written for family magazines and Adoption Today. She has written Christianity Today International's column, Grandparent's Corner and has been the past Texas Regional Director for International Fellowship. She attended Abilene Christian University and Southwestern Baptist Theological Seminary. She has taught ladies Bible classes and seminars and children's Bible classes for many years. Gail resides in Texas with her husband Neil. She has two biological children and three adopted, one from India.

7

* * * * * * * * *

---

7 Gail Gallagher Biography, GrandparentsWinning.com, 2009.

Impossible Adoption #2

We're in our sixties now, and the need for a rescue and adoption arises again. We're not giving Asa a rest. This time the adoption need is closer to home: our grandchildren, Scotty and Amber.

***

I had seen Gail faint only once and that was when she hemorrhaged after the birth of our big guy, Mitch, now age 40. He really is a big guy now—a hunk—and he was a big baby then. Big's not the word; he was huge at birth.

The hospital released Gail too soon after that difficult delivery. She screamed in pain that first night at home, and I saw purple clumps of blood the size of ping-pong balls cascading down her legs.

No 911 back then.

I scooped her in my arms and rushed to the car. Thank God, brother-in-law Roy and sister Wanda were there. While Roy cut through the back streets and Wanda prayed, I held my pale wife in my arms. We made it to the ER in time, and Gail spent two days in the hospital. Back home. All okay.

But, now it's 40 years later, and we're not in the emergency room. We're in the waiting room of family court. The clumps are still the size of ping-pong balls, except they're tears. Gail's screaming… and crying… and faints.

"You have to give Scotty and Amber back," our wimpy attorney tells us.

Scotty and Amber, our grandchildren, are the offspring of our daughter who has had serious physical and emotional problems. Son-in-law is no help. Turns out he's a renegade dad and a defector. (Let's call him R.D. for Renegade Dad.)

R.D. took off and abandoned the family. "Couldn't stand the pressure of raising a family."

(Welcome to the real world of tough love, Dude, and the daily challenges of raising a family.)

At daughter's request, we had stepped in months earlier to care for the children. We took Scotty, age 4, and Amber, age 3, home with us. Informal custody at first.

As needs intensified, it became clear that we needed to have formal, court-appointed custody and, later, adoption. Scotty and Amber came to live with us fulltime. Scotty, always precocious, started calling us Mom and Dad on his own and announced, "We're glad to be here. It's safe here." Scotty's memory was sharp. He told us tales of R.D. letting him drink a bottle of Tylenol, then being rushed to the hospital. Tales of seeing R.D. dropping Amber on her head and Amber breaking her arm, through neglect and inattention.

R.D. heard that Scotty and Amber were living with us and exploded.

No job, no money, no home, but he decides it's an affront to his manhood.

Like that nutty stepdad in Houston they showed on the national news: the ol' boy insisted on getting his three-year-old son for the weekend. But he sure wasn't going to let that stop his Saturday-night fun. He hit his usual bar on Saturday night, gave the three-year-old a Dr. Pepper and a blanket, and locked him up in the back seat while he boozed and danced.

Police and CPS came to rescue the kid. They ripped Weekend Stepdad out of the bar and charged him with neglect. His manhood was offended: "What do you mean, the safety and welfare of my son was compromised?"

Guilt and defensiveness have a way of erupting into heroic speeches and pompous actions.

R.D. finds Crusader Attorney, a zealot for father's rights. (Yes, I know in some cases it's legit and necessary... but Crusader was obsessed. "Don't confuse me with the facts." Never looked at the merits of the case.) R.D., who earlier couldn't find the money to support the family, somehow finds boxes of cash and pays crusader to bust into family court and blast the judge with blustery citations about archaic family law. Judge, tired and lazy, surrenders to the assault.

In the meantime, our lawyer (number six) was equally tired and lazy. Our Wimpy legal guy, crushed by Crusader, shrugs his shoulders and floats into the waiting room to hammer Gail and me between the eyes:

"Gotta give Scotty and Amber back."

Big guy Mitch caught Gail just before her chin smacked the greasy tile.

Mitch and I hoisted Gail onto the bench, and the horror stories of discrimination against grandparents flashed on the screen of my brain:

"Judge Biased Against 50-Something Grandparents?"[8] Yolanda and Arnold Del Bosque have taken care of their children since infancy, but when the children were eating hamburgers at the kitchen table, the state came to take them away. The judge's ruling, which led to the state's raid, wasn't prompted by any allegations of abuse and neglect, according to Child Protective Services, but apparently by the judge's belief that the Del Bosques, who are in their 50s, are too old to be parents, according to this judge.

"I don't know when the judge became God," the tearful Arnold said at the glass kitchen table smothered with legal bills and court papers aimed at fighting the judge's ruling. "I didn't know there was an age limit on grandpa or grandma helping their grandchildren."

The young children came to live with Yolanda and Arnold, her husband of 20 years, because the boys' parents struggled with drug abuse. Court appointees of Child Protective Services had filed glowing reports about the Del Bosque's parenting and their stable, nurturing home after more than a dozen visits. In spite of that, the judge ruled that 50 is old.

Wimpy's not done. He hoists a bazooka and blasts this shell: "And the judge says you've got to have 'em at Crusader's office by 4:00."

Today.

Six hours away.

We go home and tell Scotty and Amber. They cry and wail, "We don't want to leave you. We don't want to leave you."

"But we've got to take you."

8 Lisa Falkenberg, "Judge Biased Against 50-Something Grandparents?" *Houston Chronicle*, September 11, 2008.

Know pain? Take pliers and rip your fingernails out. Tape your eyes open and hit your naked wet eyeballs with a burning cigarette.

Have your appendix burst and spray its hot poison into your stomach, while you scream in belly-burning pain.

Doesn't compare with going home and telling your children, "You can't live with us anymore. The judge says you can't live here anymore. We have to take you back to the place that you're scared of."

That rat- and roach-infested place.

For months, Gail had been there, daily, at the request of R.D. and sick daughter bathing, cooking, cleaning, washing, and hauling Scotty and Amber to their doctors, playgrounds, and nursery schools. R.D. never got the message: It's the parents who do those loving chores, rather than sitting around watching television and piling bags of trash in the garage for months on end.

Climax came when R.D. made his final split. He'd defected several times, but this time we feared that CPS (Child Protective Services) could take the children away and sequester them in a foster home where none of the family would ever see them again.

Sick daughter gets sicker after R.D.'s defection. "Take me to the Scott & White Clinic[9]," she pleads. And she asks us to take Scotty and Amber home and adopt them.

Somewhere in the process, after Daughter's release from Scott & White, R.D. recruited our daughter's sympathies, using guilt, promises, and flattery to persuade her to lie about her request for us to adopt Scotty and Amber. We were forced to take Daughter to court.

That's tough.

The safety and welfare of Scotty and Amber? Or being popular with Daughter? What would you have done?

We intensified our search to find lawyers who knew family law and who knew that the safety and welfare of Scotty and Amber were preeminent. We found one specializing in custody cases and one specializing in adoption.

They got it.

---

9 Scott & White Clinic is Texas's Mayo Clinic.

Puh—leeze… don't give me this stuff about intrusive grandparents. When you're in your sixties, have bought a retirement home, are packing boxes, and have sold your business, the last thing you expect is to start all over again with two toddlers. We found out that there are millions who are starting all over again. When God honors you with an impossible task, it's for a reason, usually a reason of rescue, empowering you to secure victory for yourself and to show others how to do the same.

Following instructions from our new and competent lawyers, #7 and 8, we devoted full time to this rescue, drained our retirement savings (and everything else), and compiled eight boxes documenting:

- Scotty drinking a bottle of Tylenol and having to be rushed to the emergency room,
- Amber's accidents of being dropped on her head, resulting in red bumps the size of strawberries,
- R.D.'s reckless road habits of driving 80 miles an hour with Scotty and Amber. No seat belts. Flat tires.
- R.D. took Scotty and Amber to restaurants. Left them alone while he went to the restroom.

We lost Scotty and Amber to Crusader and R.D. for eight months. During that eight months, we assembled an armada of legal weapons. And prayed:

Help us, O God, for there is none like You
to help the weak conquer the strong.
We're here to meet this huge army of fear and worry
because we trust in You. We believe Your protective power
is with us and Scotty and Amber.
Don't let mere mortals stand against you.

We go to court and we win.

Rather, God wins. Scotty and Amber win.

Not only do we secure custody, but we secure full and final adoption. No more worries about Renegade enlisting sympathy and money from whomever to get control of Scotty and Amber and thereby relieve his guilt. We are now legally the father and legally the mother.

We dug in and learned:[10]

- In America, there are three million grandparents raising their grandchildren fulltime. This is the number on the census rolls. Experts say the number is probably closer to ten million.
- There are 5.7 million children in the United States living with a grandparent.
- There are 6.1 million grandparents who have grandchildren younger than 18 living with them.
- 730,000 grandparents with a disability are caring for their grandchildren.
- 477,000 grandparents whose income is below the poverty level are caring for their grandchildren.

Gail plowed ahead with more research and passionately took the lead in helping others.

She knew that I had thousands of clients to serve, ten speaking appointments a month, a radio show to prepare for, and upcoming interviews with Joel Osteen, Dr. Charles Stanley, Dr. Ken Cooper, Johnny Bench, Governor Mike Huckabee, and many others.

In these adoption efforts, we had peaks as sharp as jagged glass. No, we encountered MOUNTAIN peaks of jagged glass.

So will you. Get ready.

Peak One. Got to get the biological parents removed or renounce their standing. Tough. Painful. Also necessary. Victory one.

Peak Two. Pass a Child Protective Services study. You never know how regulators are going to come down. In our case, they correctly reported that the home environment we provided for Scotty and Amber was overwhelmingly safer than the one provided by R.D. Victory two.

Peak Three. Get ready for attacks and lies from relatives on the other side. R.D.'s relatives put up large amounts of money to try to block our

---

10 Source: U.S. Census Bureau

efforts to secure Scotty and Amber. They were not going to admit that their relative, R.D., was incompetent or negligent. Victory three.

Peak Four. Endurance contest. How long could we continue to do this? Twenty-one trips to the courthouse over a five-year period, with eight lawyers. Anyone who thinks grandparents enjoy "meddling" in their grandchildren's affairs is ignorant. Victory four.

Peak Five. Losing popularity with our daughter and that side of the in-law family. If you're into "approval addiction" as Joyce Meyer calls it, you can't handle this one. Victory five.

Gail was Joshua. "We most certainly can overcome."

So what if the hurdles for grandparents are high, hard, and sharp. Gail researched and wrote and spoke. Her website, www.grandparentswinning. com, is powerful and practical, equipping grandparents with legal, spiritual, and emotional strategies that work. She's the author of *Winning Custody of Grandchildren: A Grandparent's Story of Success.*[11]

When you're in your retirement years and you get thrown into the responsibility of starting a family all over again, it's, well, culture shock. You love 'em, of course. You want to help, of course.

But it's still culture shock. It's family, financial, and emotional trauma. Through it all we won. And, through her writing and speaking, Gail saw that there were millions of grandparents who needed the street smarts and daily encouragement necessary for their rescue efforts, similar to the rescue efforts of Corrie ten Boom providing safety and shelter for Jews at risk.

Our victory, and Gail's expertise, came just… in… time.

Sit down. You're not going to believe this. You'll want to read this again,
>   … and again,

>   … and again.

You've heard the saying, "When the legislature is in session, the American people cannot sleep peacefully."

Tragic and true.

---

11 Gail told me not to put this in the book, but I'm doing it anyway: She should have called her book *Don't Mess with Nana.*

For centuries, it's been understood that grandparents have the right, privilege, and opportunity to visit grandchildren. But not if Texas Bill 2084 has its way. TEXAS HOUSE BILL 2084 DENIES GRANDPARENTS ACCESS TO THEIR GRANDCHILDREN.

The bill is full of whereas's and notwithstanding's, and so be it's, but the bottom line is Section 153.434: "A grandparent may not request access to a grandchild if a court does not already have continuing exclusive jurisdiction of a suit involving the child." In other words, the court decides if you can see your grandkid. Any grandparent. Any grandkid.

And, "The grandparent may not have access to the grandchild if the child's parent who is the competent child of the grandparent opposes the suit by the grandparent seeking access." Briefly, the only way according to this bill, that a grandparent can see his or her grandchild is to file a suit to do so and hope that they win.

How did such a dangerous proposal come about and what's this bill about anyway? Gail's blog:

What is HB2084 All About Anyway?[12]

What is HB2084 all about? It's all about saying grandparents do not count anymore. It's about stripping all their rights away. And I mean all of them. In other words, it "guts" grandparents' rights.

What will this bill do to grandchildren who are abused and neglected by their parents? Not good.

There were roughly 5,000 child victims of abuse in 2008 in Tarrant county alone. If the bill is passed, it will put these children in a more than vulnerable state. If their grandparents can't get access to them, the state will take them. The state will take and shuffle them around in their already overloaded and inadequate system leaving the

---

12 Gail Gallagher, "What is HB2084 All About Anyway?" Texas Insider (www.texasinsider. org, 2009).

children longing for that warm and loving environment of their grandparents. What will they be told?

Grandparents are having to raise their grandchildren when their own children get involved in drugs, turn to alcohol, have mental illness, are incarcerated. They are not turning their heads the other way. They are sacrificing their own retirement plans and some are even going back to work. As of the 2000 U.S. Census, over 2.4 million in the U.S. were raising their grandchildren. 240,000 of them in Texas. By the way, at the same time, they have been saving the taxpayers thousands and thousands of dollars.

The homeschool community is saying that they need to be protected. The abused and neglected children in the U.S. are the ones who need to be protected.

Let in-laws settle disputes between themselves and not put these precious children at risk. The consequences will be great for the children as well as the state of Texas if this bill is passed.

My husband and I are raising our grandchildren and we know how hard it was navigating the justice system, but we got custody of them. We were determined not to give up.

I have a book coming out next month. It is primarily for grandparents who don't know what to do and don't know where to start.

Our website is www.grandparentswinning.com.

Because of Gail's courage, conviction, and compassion, she summoned statewide, then national, attention to this bill and its devastating consequences. The bill was crushed.

That bill was family swine flu, loaded with infectious power to kill families nationwide. Claiming Asa killed it.

God loves to do the impossible for everyone, including grandchildren at risk.

> Defend the cause of the weak and fatherless. Maintain the rights of the poor and oppressed. Rescue the weak and needy. Defend them from the hand of the wicked.
>
> —Psalm 82:1-4

You remember earlier in the impossible adoption of Matthew Nikilesh Gallagher, I told you that, like Asa, the victory was not just for us, but for others. Asa's conquest of the million-man army saved his army, AND saved the entire nation of Israel, part of God's overall redemptive plan. Our victory with Matthew Nikilesh Gallagher also led to the adoption of other Indian children. Ditto with our victory with Scotty and Amber. Ditto with Gail's ministry in empowering grandparents to rescue their grandchildren.

Gail writes for *Christianity Today.* Her articles also appear in Christian magazines. She writes a Bible study for grandparents called, "The Joys and Trials of Grandparents."[13] She's a contributor to *Women Ask, Women Answer*[14] (published by Thomas Nelson).

> Q: I want to cultivate a close relationship with my grandchildren. The problem is that half of them live across the country, and the ones who live nearby are school age and are constantly tied up with sports activities. What are some ways I can grow close to these grandkids in spite of the miles and the busyness?
>
> Gail's Answer: Today, the Internet makes daily communication easy and allows you to send pictures, e-cards, educational articles, and much more. Christian bookstores

---

13 Gail Gallagher, "The Joys and Trials of Grandparents," (Christianity Today, International: ChristianityBibleStudies.com)
14 Terri Gibbs, Project Manager, *Christianity Today, Women Ask, Women Answer* (Nashville: Thomas Nelson, 2007)187, 198.

are stocked with children's videos, praise CDs, character-building stories, and activity books for all ages. Some next-day shipping companies will pick up packages right at your doorstep.

Ask your children what the grandchildren get excited about and brainstorm with them with those ideas in mind. Find out if your grandchildren have reading goals at school. If they do, you might want to contribute a book for that project. For your grandchildren nearby, offer to provide homework relief for their parents. If you have taken an especially interesting trip, have a pet, or enjoy a special hobby such as gardening, send your grandchildren pictures in a small album so they can share in your life, too.

Q: When my husband and I envisioned retirement, we pictured white sandy beaches or a beautiful retirement village. Instead we've made a complete U-turn. We're raising our granddaughter! I feel good about the decision we've made to parent her, but sometimes I feel disappointed that the retirement years aren't what I thought they'd be. How can I have a better attitude?

Gail's Answer: Many of today's grandparents are abandoning their retirement dreams and returning to the world of report cards, temper tantrums, and sleepovers. When grandparents take on the role of parents to their grandchildren, they know that there are many unseen challenges to face.

Amanda is a single woman in her forties whose adult daughter is on drugs. Amanda doesn't hesitate to rescue her granddaughter from a potentially dangerous situation. She has had her granddaughter for two years and they make quite a team. Amanda's seven-year-old granddaughter has been richly blessed and saved from a life of trouble. Amanda, who has MS and is in a wheelchair, has a loving companion and a great helper. Amanda had all kinds of valid reasons to say no to taking in her granddaughter, yet she chose to do what she felt God was asking her to do.

There are countless stories of grandparents of all ages who are making U-turns and caring for their grandchildren in difficult circumstances. It can often feel discouraging. But remember that no matter how impossible a problem looks, there is a solution rooted in our heavenly Father.

* * * * * * * *

Update

The Rescue Expands

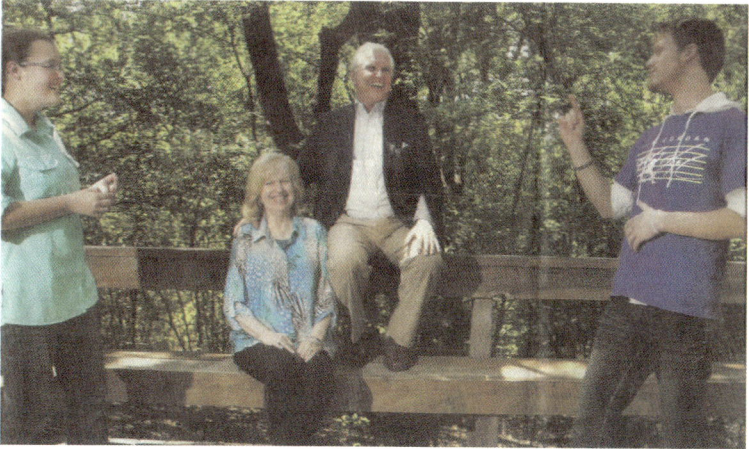

Just in…

Dallas Morning News learns of the plight of grandchildren and our rescue successes for ourselves and others.

Tuesday, August 18, 2014:

Grand Love, great sacrifice
Grandparents face challenges the second time around in familiar role of raising kids

Gail and Neil Gallagher, both 73, have no plans to retire. They should be enjoying some hard-earned time off, but like many other grandparents across the country, they were swept up in a growing trend: raising grandkids.

The sudden lifestyle change can create unexpected hardships—emotional, financial and physical—as grandparents bring up another generation of children.

The numbers are staggering. One in 10 children in the U.S. lives with a grandparent, according to the National Kinship Alliance for Children…

"…Grandparents can't imagine not keeping their grandkids in the family, but they often don't know where to get help," she [Gail Gallagher] says.

When their grandson and granddaughter first came to live with them as toddlers, Gail Gallagher of North Richland Hills says she and her husband floundered.

"We didn't know where to turn. We didn't know what to do. We didn't know how to pick an attorney," says Gail, who quit seminary so she could focus on Scott and Amber, whom the couple eventually adopted as their daughter struggled with bipolar disorder.

After futilely searching for resources, Gallagher finally found a helpful book, Charlotte Hardwick's *Win Your Child Custody War*. She called to thank the publisher , who persuaded her to self-publish her own experiences. *Grandparents Winning Custody of Grandchildren* (Pale Horse Publishing, 2010) was just the beginning of the Gallaghers' outreach.

"Grandparents have to waste $100,000 sometimes trying to get their grandkids and to prove they're capable," she says. "Some laws have got to be changed. There are so many grandparents who have lost their grandkids back to parents who are not responsible."

Gail now serves on the board of the National Kinship Alliance for Children, where she fields dozens of calls.

"They cry on my shoulder all the time," she says. "A lot of them need financial help. A lot of times they just want to talk to somebody. There are just so many bad stories."

Gail hears firsthand how grandparents on fixed incomes struggle to stay afloat financially. The median income for U.S. grandparents raising grandchildren without parental backing was $33,000, according to the 2010 U.S. Census Bureau's American Community Survey...

..."You see how happy they are," Gail says. "They're thriving and they're not in harm's way anymore. If they had been left with her, I can't imagine where in the world they would be now."[15]

Praying Asa ignites many "impossible" rescue missions including those sometimes sparked by an angel.

---

15 Kathleen Green, "Grand love, great sacrifice," *Dallas Morning News: Senior Living,* August 2014, 15-20.

1D - An Angel Visits

1D - An Angel Visits

I've been in this building 23 years, and I had never seen this woman before. She sat on the couch in the front lobby next to the elevator. Her shrieks and sobs bounced up and down the stairs and ricocheted down the hallways hosting offices for lawyers, contractors, insurance agencies, real estate offices, and financial counseling offices. Like mine.

I saw her shoulders heaving up and down in cadence with her shrieks and sobs. *Not anyone in this building, for sure.*

I snapped the sharp-angled white handkerchief from my breast pocket and extended it to her. "Here, ma'am. Take this. Anything I can do to help?" I snapped the handkerchief open and shook it to its full length, now a hand towel.

"I'll never see him again. Never. I'll never." She took the handkerchief, laid it flat against her soggy face with two palms pressing against her cheekbones.

"Who?"

"My son."

"Did you have an accident? Did your s—? May I sit down?"

"No, upstairs. His lawyer… said, Get used to it. Jason's his."

"His, who?"

She still hadn't looked up at me. She screamed through the handkerchief: "My boyfriend. We've split. He took Jason."

"Jason's your s-son? I'm guessing here."

"Yes. Mario is my boyfriend. Might still be up there in the lawyer's office. Got to the daycare before I did…" Her cell rang. "No, Mom. No, Mom, I can't talk now. I can't. I'll call you back."

"I'm still guessing. Mario went to daycare? Got there before you did and got Jason out, and then took him what—to his house? And then got some lawyer to stonewall you? Something like that?"

"Yuh, we were together again just a few days. Mario hit me, slapped Jason around and left. Said he'd get even."

"Even for what? By the way, I'm Dr. Gallagher. Have an office upstairs. What's your name? And what was the reason that Mario got so angry?"

"Toni. Drunks don't need reasons!" she snapped, sat up, and lowered the handkerchief. "What do you care? Who are you?"

"Do you want help or not? Do you have custody?" I asked, flipping my wrist over and staring at my watch. *Do I have time for this?*

"Custody? What for? Mario's just a boyfriend. Used to be. Been living in and out for a few years. Left a note for me at the daycare. 'Go see lawyer Kendall.'"

I looked at my watch again. 10:14. My clients had been waiting upstairs since 10:00. I flipped my cell and hit the speed dial. "Laura, I'm downstairs. I assume Dr. and Mrs. Wells are still there? I'll be there... Honestly, I'll be there real quick. Put in that DVD of *America's Greatest Moments*. Tell them I apologize. Five minutes. Five minutes, Yes, I know, I know. They've waited two and a half months for this appointment. I know. They've got the $750,000. I know. I know."

I returned to Toni.

"Do you have a lawyer, Toni?"

"Won't do any good. The lawyer upstairs said he's got him and he's moving out of state, maybe already did. I don't know what Mario told that lawyer."

I flipped my cell open again and hit the speed dial to call my attorney. "Brad, do you know a good family lawyer?"

"David Walsh. Here's his number."

I hit the red button, ending the call. I hit the green button and dialed in David Walsh.

Got him.

I briefed him, and he asked me to put Toni on the phone. She exploded into sobs and her rapid rat-tat-tat-tat of facts. She handed the phone back to me.

"I need a $3,500 retainer to get this started. Send her over. We'll see what we can do. If she's telling the truth, we can help her and need to do it immediately before this guy gets too far."

$Thirty-five hundred dollars? I don't even know this woman.

"Stay here, Toni."

I ran upstairs, praying all the time. I escorted Dr. and Mrs. Wells to a conference room with profuse apologies. "Be right back."

I wrote a check to attorney David Walsh, stuffed it in an envelope, sealed it, and handed it to Laura. "Laura, there's a gal downstairs by the elevator, name is Toni. Give her this envelope, point out to her that on the front I've put David Walsh's name and address. She's talked to him. She knows who he is. She's going to take this to him."

I met with Dr. and Mrs. Wells, completed the estate plan, and set up their retirement accounts.

Two-fifty p.m., comes a call from David Walsh's office. "I talked to Toni. We sent CPS and the Dallas Police to make a little visit to Mario. Essentially, Mario kidnapped Jason. Toni's got Jason back. Mario's in jail, and he probably won't be harassing Toni again, if ever.

Thank you, Lord.

And Toni never talked to me again. Never heard from her. No call. No visit. No "thank you."

And I know why.

It finally hit me. God set it up. Yes, He did.

God sent Toni and her problems to me, I believe, just like He sent an angel to wrestle with Jacob. And just like the opportunities for dramatic service that He sends to all believers from time to time.

"God, yes, <u>You</u> Lord. You wanted her to get help, but You also wanted to wrestle with my faith. You wanted to see if I was going to walk the walk. You wanted to see if I was too busy to interrupt my business to take care of someone who needed unconditional caring and radical trust. You wanted to see just how tight I was holding on to my money and time."

Earlier that day, I remembered saying, "God make my life a miracle of Your service. There's a million-man army out there, and I need your overwhelming strength and compassion to conquer it. If You want to use me, I'm ready."

Warning: <u>Never </u>say the above prayer unless you're ready for a rollercoaster ride of risks and actions—which are w-a-y out of your comfort zone. And you will also feel the thrill of divine victories.

My profs in the cloistered classrooms of our Ivy League towers, chafed at my embracing those divine truths. You'll see.

* * * * * * * * *

1E - "No One's Ever Done That Before"

1E - "No One's Ever Done That Before"

"At MIT, science and technology are the gods we serve."[16]

—MIT Professor

W. NEIL GALLAGHER

GRADU DOCTORIS PHILOSOPHIAE
CANDITATUM COMPETENTEM ET EXAMINE USITATO
PROBATUM PRAECIPUE IN
PHILOSOPHIA
ET HUIC OMNIA PRIVILEGIA ET HONORES ET IURA ET
INSIGNIA IIS
AD HUNC GRADUM EVECTIS PERTINENTIA FRUENDA DEDIT
CUIUS IN REI TESTIMONIUM NOS HIS LITTERIS
UNIVERSITATIS
SIGILLO MUNITIS NOMINA NOSTRA SUBSCRIPSIMUS
DATUM IN SOLEMNIBUS ACADEMICIS PROVIDENTIAE
HABITIS DIE
PRIMO IUNII ANNOQUE DOMINI NOSTRI MCMLXXXI

That's the way the degrees look from my Ivy institution. And how they deliver the commencement greetings. In Latin. Been doing it for about two and a half centuries.

And that's the Latin parchment they tried to rip from me.

---

16 Michael Guillen, *Can a Smart Person Believe in God?* (Nashville: Thomas Nelson, Inc, 2004) 3.

My dissertation examiners were outraged by my arguments and my conclusions.

Were they jealous? Maybe: I was the only Ivy League Ph.D.-to-be who had published in scholarly journals *before* entrance to graduate school, and I may have been the only one who eclipsed his examiners by publishing in scholarly journals they had not published in. Or maybe it was just the arrogant attitude of the profession generally, as summed by Dr. Phil:

> No less painfully, there had been the days, weeks, and months of dealing with a variety of insecure, "emotionally interesting" professors, many of them white-coated Napoleons who were all too eager to wield the power of their petty fiefdoms. Their torments had culminated in that unforgettable final year, when he [Dr. Phil] had walked the halls at school and put in his time at the hospital, armed with a signed letter of resignation on his clipboard, daring just one more anal-retentive, power-hungry mentor-turned-tormentor to say so much as "boo" to him.
>
> In spite of it all, and as surprised as anyone who knew him, here he stood. He remembered one of his favorite profs telling him he would never make it because he had an "attitude" and refused to "kiss ass." He was told, "You have too many options in your life to put up with this fiasco of dysfunction, you aren't near desperate enough to tolerate the abuse!" Yet here he was. One by one, the department heads had signed off on his final requirements, shaken his hand, and congratulated him on bearing the highest degree in his profession. Doctor—wow! He knew how proud his dad was going to be. This phone call would be a huge step closer to a father's dream come

true: father and son, both doctors, practicing together, side by side![17]

Here we were in this historic room, 220 years old, adorned with Gilbert Stuart's originals of Washington. Across the yard was the administration building used by Washington to house troops during the Revolutionary War. Murals of American business legends adorned the classrooms and buildings adjacent to this historic hall: Rockefeller Library, Carnegie Auditorium, Vanderbilt Hall.

My examiners told me, in effect, I was not worthy of their signatures concluding my four years of doctoral studies and crowned with this dissertation on *The Therapy of Responsibility*.[18] It was sophomoric, they whined. "Go to a junior high school and teach there," they scolded. "You won't make it in the university."

I returned to my car that chilly March day and flipped the seat backwards. I turned on the heat and raged. My stomach roiled, and my hands were sheets of sweat. What was I going to do? I knew that my propositions, arguments, and conclusions were solid. They had been tested in the academic rigor of solid publications and earlier debates. My argument:

a) Free will is a gift to men and women by a benevolent, transcendent, loving God.

b) When exercising free will, men and women enjoy the dignity and independence unique to the human race.

c) Because men and women are free-will creatures, it is a compliment to hold them responsible for their decisions and actions. This is true freedom. Metaphysically sound, morally imperative, and emotionally therapeutic. Furthermore, the practice of blaming others was irrational and self-destructive, and the philosophy of determinism was a vacuous and dehumanizing world view.

---

17 Phil McGraw, *Self Matters: Creating Your Life from the Inside Out* (New York: Free Press, 2004), 3-4.
18 Later retitled *The Concept of Blame: Utilitarian Blame and Its Consequences.*

This three-fold premise argument had been documented (1) in the medical community by Dr. Karl Menninger, eminent psychiatrist and author of *The Blue Bird on the Dung Heap* and *Man Against Himself*; (2) in the psychological community by Dr. William Glasser in his book *Reality Therapy* and in his hands-on successes with patients; and (3) in the philosophical community by Dr. Francis Schaeffer, *Time Magazine*'s "missionary to the intellectual" and author of *Escape from Reason*.

How to describe this defeat to my family?

A hundred-and-ten-thousand dollars in graduate school debts, fighting and scraping for that Ivy Ph.D. Four years of fulltime study, one year of writing a dissertation, and living on starvation wages supporting a wife and three children.

My wife knew up front (and so did I) that I had strategically chosen the most liberal discipline in the most liberal university. My stated goal was to teach in a state university or Ivy League university to practice true academic freedom, i.e. to show "the other side of the news." That other side was to show that the Biblical propositions of truth were consistent with epistemology, metaphysics, and axiology. Actually, I argued, the Biblical propositions of truth are the only ones that tie all disciplines together consistently, rigorously, and therapeutically.

In the words of Francis Schaeffer: "Biblical truth is the truth that gives a unity to all of knowledge and all of life."[19]

Why this feeling of shock?

I knew ahead of time that my dissertation committee was made up of atheists. One was a celebrated humanist and the state chairman of the ACLU. Naïvely, I thought they would be objective and rational and see that my dissertation, *The Therapy of Responsibility*, was solid. I had proven my scholarly achievements in the arena of publishing. And I had mastered my graduate courses and defended my papers in my courses in *Kant, Wittgenstein, Whitehead, Philosophy of Punishment, Philosophy and Psychiatry, Philosophy of History, Philosophy of Education, Symbolic Logic, Philosophy of Science*, and a dozen others.

---

19 Francis A. Schaeffer, *The Complete Works of Francis A. Schaeffer, a Christian World View*, Vol. 5 (Wheaton, IL: Crossway Books 1982) 251

In this twelfth hour, it appeared that my examiners not only hated my Biblical perspective but, well, hated me. They viewed me, as Bill Buckley summed it from his experience at an Ivy icon, as the "barbarian who invaded the temple."[20]

I had argued: ideas lead to beliefs, beliefs to actions, actions to consequences. And the idea that we live in a universe of chaos leads to chaotic living and cruel treatment of people.

Committee didn't agree.

And now it's climax time: I dropped my head on my right shoulder and shut off the engine. After several moments of silence, I prayed, "This is a million-man army, God, and I'm not exaggerating, and this is not any type of cliché."

> LORD, there is no one like You
>> to help the powerless against the mighty.
> Help us, LORD our God,
>> for we rely on You,
> and in Your Name
>> we have come against this vast army.
> LORD, You are our God;
>> do not let mere mortals
>> prevail against You.

---

20 My goal was similar to that spoken by Harold Abrahams in *Chariots of Fire*. "Here am I in the finest university in the land… in these hallowed halls. And those in charge stalk them with jealousy and power."

"So what are you going to do, just grin and bear it?" asks Aubrey,

"No… I'm going to take them on one by one and run them off their feet."

My perspective was then (and still is) that there is no rational or compassionate basis to atheism or any of its phony names, humanism, skepticism, agnosticism, etc. I will take them on one by one to show them, the professors and their adoring students, that there is much more to truth than academic applause or popular sentiment.

I ripped the keys from the ignition and snapped the seatbelt from my hips. My feet slapped the 200-year -old cobblestone street as the tiny colonial houses whizzed by as I sprinted to the campus quad.

Heaving and sweating, I marched into the administration office and demanded to see the university president, Dr. Howard Swearer. Heck, I figured, if Columbia students can commandeer a president's office with guns and threats for 24 hours, I could go in directly and peacefully and ask for an audience. And, I told the secretary, I would wait in the office, for weeks if necessary.

I received my audience, I presented my case, I documented my credentials, and I was awarded a new committee.

No guarantees, of course.

"No one's ever done that before," came the astonishing observation.

The new committee examined my dissertation with penetrating questions, solicited a public forum to review it, and found my arguments unassailable. So months later, on an early June day I walked across that historic lawn with my family watching. I felt the soft brown and red velvet of the Ph.D. hood rub against the base of my neck as I descended the podium.

And God wasn't through with me yet.

"God, what do I do with this experience? What to do with this knowledge and victory?"

I wrote "Ivy Rot," an essay on the history and trends of the Ivies.

I began by interviewing Ann Coulter on my show, *Your Family Matters*. On the cover of *Time*, as "Ms. Right" and labeled "the most loved—and hated—woman in America," Ann, an Ivy alum herself, recalled the story of John Stossel's visit to my beloved and "open-minded" Brown University.

Stossel, the celebrated host of *20/20*, spoke on the topic of political correctness… "political bullying," he called it. And they pulled the plug on him. Literally. A gang of students pulled the plug on the mics and speakers. No one in the university rejoined the plugs, rebuked the students, or repaired the offense.

Stossel's confrontation with political bullying and wanton censorship is one of many:

- Columbia

  Dinesh D'Souza, author of *Letters to a Young Conservative, The Enemy At Home: The Cultural Left and Its Responsibility for 9/11*, and *What's So Great about Christianity*, was greeted at Columbia University with hateful mobs threatening him and spitting on him. Columbia administration refused to discipline the protestors and attempted to ban his speech from the campus. Prior to his coming to speak, Columbia newspapers billed the upcoming conference as racist, sexist, and a threat to civil rights.

- **Cornell**

  In 1988, a public burning of the conservative *Cornell Review* was conducted. That also was "justified" by perverting the First Amendment. (Ann Coulter had been a writer for the *Cornell Review* during her undergraduate days there.)

- **Yale**

  Students stole the campus paper *Light and Truth,* because *Light and Truth* criticized the promotion of a safe sex program. The so-called "safe sex" program promoted risky sexual behavior in the guise of sexual liberation. Ellen Key criticized the program's encouragement of one-night stands. Too conservative, obviously. Too moral. Too absolute. So Yale students, with approval of the administration, stole the papers.

No surprise then to learn that ninety percent of the instructors in the Art & Science department in places like Harvard, Cornell, and Brown are registered Democrats or members of other Left-leaning parties. Eighty percent of Ivy League professors confess to voting for Democratic presidential candidate Al Gore in 2000.

How did this censorship toward the Christian perspective and hatred toward absolutes develop where, presumably, the best and brightest study, and where free thought and free speech flourish?

The Ivies began as academies to train Christian leaders: Brown for Baptists, Harvard for Puritans, Princeton for Presbyterians, Yale for Congregationalists, etc. ABC News Science Correspondent and Harvard Professor Michael Guillen summed it when he said:

> As for the New World, one of the first things Puritans did when they arrived was set up Harvard College, the oldest university in North America. Afterwards, Christians of every denomination—from Roman Catholic, Baptist, and Congregationalist to Episcopalian, Methodist, and the Church of Christ—established what are today many of our most prestigious academic establishments.[21]

That respect for the Biblical perspective, and the practice of Biblical compassion, continued for several centuries.

Charles Seymour, president of Yale: "I call on all members of the faculty as members of a thinking body freely to recognize the tremendous validity and power of the teachings of Christ in our life and death struggle against the force of selfish materialism. Yale is dedicated to the training of spiritual leaders. We betray our trust if we fail to explore the various ways in which the youth who come to us may learn to appreciate spiritual values whether by the example of our own lives or through the cogency of our philosophical arguments. The simple and direct way is through the maintenance and upbuilding of the Christian religion as a vital part of university life."

How did we go from that intellectual honesty, common sense, and spiritual wisdom to censorship and prejudice? The descent was gradual: the story of the frog sitting in cool water. His skin adapts to the cool water. Gradually, the water heats and his skin adapts to the warm water. Eventually, the water boils. His skin adapts to the boiling water, and he boils alive.

---

21 Michael Guillen, *Can a Smart Person Believe in God?* (Nashville: Thomas Nelson, Inc. 2004) 26.

This descent into censorship and prejudice began with the confusion between academic freedom and academic anarchy. Academic freedom allows for any question to be asked. It does not mean that *any* answer is truth. Nor does it mean that all solutions are good and equal.

That's <u>anarchy</u>, an academic word for saying, "That's WACKO."

Nor does it mean that the people who foot the bill for the university have to support opposing points of view which may be, in fact, destructive. No one can <u>force</u> you to feed the mouth which continually bites your hand. Common sense.

Bill Buckley in *God and Man at Yale*[22]: "If I knew that a professor were preaching genocide, I should think it a duty, if I were able, to prevent him, even though his views were being adequately refuted in the next classroom." And, "The idea of having a flat world is not equally good with the idea of acknowledging that the earth is round." A flat-world view is obviously destructive to the progress of science, and its errors would have to be exposed.

When you pose a question or raise a challenge, you can express doubt, but that's not the same thing as saying that academic freedom requires that all proffered answers are valuable or worthy.

Nor does it require—or even allow— for the *a priori* censorship of the classical truths of free will and moral responsibility.

Common-sense conclusions:

a) The Ivies began as Christian universities.

b) Therefore, the Christian perspective should be included as part of teaching and life of the students.

c) (1) At the very least, the Christian perspective should not be maligned or censored.

(2) The irony is that, in the Ivies, many religious and philosophical perspectives are explored as being tenable, but the only perspective routinely denigrated is the Christian perspective. This is rank prejudice and Nazi-like mind control.

---

22 William F. Buckley, Jr., *God & Man at Yale* (Washington, D.C.: Regnery Gateway Editions, 1986, p. 89

d) The Ivies prosper through the efforts of entrepreneurs funding the private institutions; therefore, the benefits of compassionate capitalism and the contributions of the Ivies' spiritual founders, business leaders, and entrepreneurial benefactors should be acknowledged and praised.

e) At the very least, compassionate capitalism and its historic contributions (and present benefits) should NOT be misrepresented or ignored.

Fact is: The economics departments today in many American universities (Ivies and state) are Socialist. Talk about biting the hand that feeds you! With saber-like teeth, the professors rip off your shoulder if you praise capitalism or mention moral absolutes.

***

If alleged neutrality, academic freedom, and openness to opposing views means there are NO ABSOLUTES, we can say…

- Hitler's *Mein Kampf* is morally equal to Francis Schaeffer's *The God Who Is There*.
- *The Negro as Beast* (a 19th century racist manual) is morally equal to Martin Luther's King's *Letter from the Birmingham Jail*.
- Machiavelli's *On Power* is morally equal to Jesus' *Beatitudes*.
- *Kristallnacht* is morally equal to Christmas Eve.
- And Bernie Madoff's ponzi schemes are morally equal to Billy Graham's crusades.

Bernie and Billy.

No difference.

No absolute standard. No moral arbiter. No judge.

Talking about Billy… that's the problem.

Billy said it a million times (and the academics hate it):

- "The Bible says,
- the Bible says,

- the Bible says."

And another million times, "Jesus said, 'I am the way and the truth and the life.'"

OK, Billy, you can talk about Jesus. And it's OK to see Jesus as a divine pal passing out hugs and kisses, but this stuff about "the Bible is God's truth," and "I am the way and the truth and the life," and "No one comes to the Father except through Me," and "He who has seen Me has seen the Father." That's absolute, and because it's absolute, it's absolutely dangerous and, of course, un-American.

Crush it.

Gradually… very gradually… leaders in the Ivies came, with trembling, to recognize that with regard to Christ, the Bible, and Truth, only two positions exist:

(1. There are rules.

(2. There are no rules.

Ivy leaders, and their media mouthpieces, practice the latter. My university colleagues scream at this conclusion and will censor the book—or at least smear it—hoping few will read it with an open mind.

"There are no rules!"

"Everything is relative!"

This engine of moral relativism continues to be fueled by their academic devotion to the picture of the elephant and six blind men.

You've seen it.

It's in the intro chapters of every college text in philosophy, psychology, sociology, communications, and literature. Six blind men explore an elephant's body:

1. The first blind man feels the trunk. "I know what an elephant is. An elephant is a big, thick snake, narrow at the bottom and thick at its head."
2. The second blind man feels the leg. "I know what an elephant is. An elephant is a tree, wide and rough. Big, thick tree."
3. The third blind man feels the ears. "I know what an elephant is. An elephant is a tall bush with large, leathery leaves."

4. The fourth blind man feels the tusk. "I know what an elephant is. An elephant is a smooth, curved stick."

5. The fifth blind man feels the tail. "I know what an elephant is. The elephant is a branch, thick up and down, and it's coarse, but it's a branch."

6. The sixth blind man feels the belly. "I know what an elephant is. An elephant is the side of a mountain. It's a warm hill on the side of a mountain. I can feel its ridges between my fingernails, and as far as I stretch, that hill extends."

With this metaphor and picture, academics gleefully tell us that truth depends entirely upon the experience of the beholder. Case closed.

False.

What the metaphor overlooks is that THE SIX PEOPLE FEELING THE ELEPHANT ARE BLIND. Blind.

But we are not blind. We are sentient and cerebral creatures, with free will. We have eyes, and ears, and brains. We can sift through competing offers of truth and discern if there really is such a thing as an objective elephant.

The metaphor of the elephant, preached by mouth and in print to adoring students, proves the OPPOSITE of the intended delusion. To anyone who prides himself or herself on carrying the light of intelligence and common sense, elephants are REAL and devoid of anyone's subjective experience.

Relativism is the norm, insist the academic leaders, and this fact does not diminish moral responsibility. The abiding rule for moral context is REASON, they say. That's all there is. That's all there ever was. Reason. That's what the universe, or divine force, or energia, or whatever you want to call it gives us.

Reason.

Reason is the only rule and guide of conduct that anyone needs.

Wonderful.

Whose reason?

Perfectly reasonable to Hitler to cleanse Germany of Jews, since, according to him, Jews caused Germany's money problems and diluted Aryan purity. Seemed reasonable to Eichman to herd those Jews on boxcars, because it was perfectly reasonable to obey your leader.

Whose reason?

Perfectly reasonable in medieval China to stuff girls' feet in tiny boxes, so the feet wouldn't grow. Tiny feet equals beautiful. (Tiny feet also meant crippled for life... but that didn't meet the reasonable standard back then.)

Was "perfectly reasonable" for an aspiring Mafia don to fulfilll his obligatory murder in order to be embraced in The Family. That was the reasonable standard.

Whose reason?

"Dr. Gallagher, you know what I mean. Any action is reasonable as long as it doesn't hurt others."

And what does THAT mean? When it comes to self-preservation, or, in some cases, personal convenience, either they get hurt or I get hurt. The mafia set of "ethics" is illuminating: kill or be killed. Meets the rule of reason and self-preservation, for them.

Either they get hurt or I get hurt.

Eat or be eaten.

Guess who wins.

Not only is banishing ethical absolutes mandatory for the Ivies and their followers, but common sense must also be banished.

Do not appeal to common sense. Way too revealing and way too embarrassing.

Common sense principles which offend the Ivies (Common sense equals CS):

Common

Sense One. He who pays the piano player picks the tune.

> The students, parents, and alumni who pay for an education have the right and obligation to comment on the quality of the education, and to recommend improvements, and to withhold funds if recommendations are ignored.

"Not so," say the profs. "We are the tutorial and paternalistic dictators. We are morally superior. Send us your checks and shut up."

Henry Coffin Sloane, the misanthropic and America-hater chaplain of Yale University, spilled the beans when he said, "Why leave the education up to a bunch of alumni and parents who are nothing but a bunch of boobs?" The boobs Sloane was talking about are the doctors, lawyers, teachers, engineers, mothers, CEOs, and thousands of other alumni who place a high value on comprehensive education and who have more practical life experience than the dictatorial professors, and who, by the way, send money to support the universities.

David Horowitz's *New York Times* best-seller indicted the mis-education and arrogance in the Ivies specifically (and universities generally) when he said, "Remember Ward Churchill, the professor who compared the victims of the September 11 terrorist attacks to Nazis who deserved what they got. You thought he was bad. Wild academics aren't the exception. They're legion, and far from being harmless, they spew violent anti-Americanism, preach anti-Semitism, and cheer on the killing of American soldiers and civilians, all the while collecting tax dollars and tuition fees to indoctrinate our children."[23]

Common Sense Two. You eat only what you harvest, and you can harvest only what you plant. If you didn't grow it, it's not yours to harvest. If you didn't grow it, it's not yours to eat. If others planted it, you answer to them.

---

23 David Horowitz, *The Professors: The 101 Most Dangerous Academics in America* (Washington, DC, Regnery Publishing, 2007) page #.

Common

Sense Three. Academics insist, "There is no such thing as absolute truth." I asked a colleague in my department one time, "Are you sure there is no such thing as absolute truth?" His answer: "Absolutely."

Physics professor Dr. Allen Sokal joined me in exposing the dangers and stupidity of relativism. He submitted an article to the New York publication *Social Text*. He used a deliberate parody arguing, "Without the slightest evidence of argument... physical reality is at the bottom of social and linguistic construct." He argued that reality—reality itself—was a social and linguistic construct. After witnessing that the editors regarded this as an academically respectable piece and actually published the article, he then announced the purpose of his experiment, and he added, "Anyone who believes that the laws of physics are mere social and linguistic conventions is invited to try transgressing these conventions from the windows of my apartment. I live on the 21st floor." He went on to say that he was angered by "the proliferation of this particular kind of nonsense and sloppy thinking, that denies the existence of objective reality, or when challenged admits their existence but downplays their relevance. This silliness emanates from the self-proclaimed Left." And he added, "Theorizing about the social construction of reality won't help us find an effective treatment for AIDS or devise strategies for global warming, nor can we combat false ideas in history, sociology, economics, and politics if we reject the notions of truth and falsity."[24]

24 Alan Sokal, "A Physicists Experiments with Cultural Studies," *Lingua Franca*, May-June 1966.

Commenting on Sokal's article, attorney David Limbaugh observed, "Sokal's experiment and findings are fitting lament for the deplorable moral academic condition of many of our college campuses, which is the byproduct of the American cultural elite's rejection of absolute truth and traditional values in favor of post-modern relativism." [25]

Is there a need for absolute truth?

Imagine a professor saying a 13-inch ruler is as good as a 9-inch ruler, and they're both equally as good as a 12-inch ruler. Or that a 73-minute clock is as good as a 45-minute clock, and they're both as good as a 60-minute clock.

Common sense demands absolute truth and absolute standards. The decline into academic anarchy (the dissolution of absolute truth) began with the arbitrary division between physics and metaphysics.

Physics, accessible to the five senses, is presumably the only area where truth can be documented and verified; therefore, the principles of physics (and science generally) represent absolute truth… a luxury denied to metaphysics.

Metaphysics, which includes ethics, is not accessible to the five senses and therefore is non-verifiable.

So what?

Here's the so what: METAPHYSICAL PRINCIPLES DO DISPLAY VERIFIABLE TRUTHS…

a) Good decisions lead to good actions, which lead to good consequences. That is a reality of human life that transcends the empirical. Daily life documents this absolute truth. It's called sowing—and—reaping.

25 David Limbaugh, *Persecution: How Liberals Wage War Against Christianity* (Washington, D.C.: Regnery Publishing, Inc., 2003) 140.

b) People were made to give love unconditionally and to receive love unconditionally. That is a given. People who deny that truth collapse into dysfunction, violence, depression, or suicide, or all four. That need to give and receive love is a metaphysical reality... an absolute fact.

Common Sense Four. All ideas are not equal, despite the ranting of those guarding academic turf. Lynching blacks is not an equally good idea with giving blacks their right to vote. Castrating your enemies is not an equally good idea with the principle of forgiving your enemies. The Islamic practice of forced clitorectomies is not an equally good idea with the idea of vaccinating children against disease. The Hindu practice of suttee, throwing a live widow in the funeral pyre with her dead husband, is not an equally good idea with Mother Teresa's charity to the sick and dying.

Good ideas offer themselves up for good beliefs, and good beliefs offer themselves up for good actions. It's imperative to recognize good ideas and champion them. It's equally imperative to recognize bad ideas, expose them, and correct them.

Ideas lead to beliefs, lead to actions, lead to consequences.

Ideas → Beliefs → Actions → Consequences.

A. Bible IDEA: All men and women are created equal. (No male or female... all are one in Christ Jesus... We have the same Heavenly Father, etc.)

→ BELIEF embraced by Ronald Reagan: "Inside the Bible's pages lie the answers to all the problems that mankind has ever known. I hope people everywhere will read and study the

Bible. The Bible can touch our hearts, order our minds, and refresh our souls."

→ ACTION: "Mr. Gorbachev, tear down these walls."

→ CONSEQUENCE: 100 million people freed.

→ Bible IDEA: Sow what you reap. The diligent shall prosper.

→ BELIEF embraced by Ronald Reagan: Allow the American worker to reap more of what he has sown. Get the government off his back.

→ ACTION:

- Lower government regulation.

→ CONSEQUENCES:

- Millions of new jobs were created.
- America was restored to international business leadership.
- Ushered in the greatest bull market in American history.

Common Sense Five. When you expose evil, you're the good guy, not the bad guy.

Right?

Wrong.

Academics have it backwards. If you're the guy who says the emperor has no clothes, you're the bad guy. Consider the case of Yale darling Bill Clinton and prosecutor Kenneth Starr. Kenneth Starr, a distinguished scholar and law professor, was assigned the task of documenting the sensational case of Monica Lewinsky's seduction by Bill Clinton.

Kenneth Starr became the bad guy.

Starr was characterized as vindictive, shallow, and arbitrary. Starr was portrayed as a showman who was performing before a Grand Jury. The fact that

Bill Clinton abused his power and refused to control his sexual appetite was ignored by the university and much of the media.

CS Six. The university should be a leader. "Leader" means to establish a vision, a vision that is positive and progressive, uplifting and honoring. A university should enact those attitudes and actions to bring that vision to fruition and to promote future leaders to do the same. Universities should not be citadels for cynicism, sedition, and censorship.

But when they are, hit them head-on by claiming the prayer of Asa and taking on these million-man armies with dispatch, accuracy, compassion, and courage.

Come on… Claim Asa with me and claim the return of academe to its Biblical heritage, scholarly rigor, and <u>true</u> open-mindedness. Pray for these academic leaders drowning in a swamp of darkness. Here's their thinking:

1. I cannot admit that there is absolute truth because… well, because… *I* don't have this absolute truth. And if there's absolute truth out there and I don't have it, that means that I am wrong. That is an affront to my pride and lifestyle.

2. I certainly cannot admit that there is absolute moral truth. Because if there is absolute moral truth out there and I don't know it and I don't obey it, then I am immoral.

3. And I know that I am <u>not</u> an immoral person. I send my $250 a year to UNICEF. Twice a year, I bag up my used clothes and worn out appliances and give them to the Leukemia Association.

4. I even volunteer once a month at the food bank.

It's amazing how people, ignorant of <u>God's</u> light of reason, create their own standards of reason and morality. In their darkness, they ignore the truth of Isaiah 22:11.

You built a reservoir between the two walls for the water of the Old Pool, but you did not look to the One who made it or have regard for the One who planned it long ago.

—Isaiah 22:11

Paraphrased: "You looked and you looked and you looked, but you never looked at Him who gave you this university in the first place, and you never once consulted the One who had long plans for this university."

The founders of American universities understood this truth:

But the man who loves God is known by God.

—1 Cor. 8:3

What the Ivies (and other academics) have forgotten is the difference between information, knowledge, and wisdom.

a) <u>Information</u> is facts. We are flooded with facts thanks to today's Internet world.

b) <u>Knowledge</u> is facts put to use. Nothing helpful here. Hitler's henchmen were very knowledgeable, the most brilliant scientists and military men in Germany.

  Hackers and stalkers and scammers are very good with knowledge.

c) But <u>wisdom</u>—ah, <u>wisdom</u>. Wisdom is knowledge, based upon the absolute certainty of moral facts, put to use in the service of God for benevolent, uplifting service to men and women.

* * * * * * * * *

1F - Ambush on ABC

HOW TO STOP THE PORNO PLAGUE

- Have you been embarrassed by the magazine covers at your local supermarket?
- Do you steer your kids away from the literature displays at your drugstore?
- Are you revolted by the increase of pornography in print, picture and film?

ARE YOU ANGRY ABOUT THE DEGENERATE DISTORTION OF SEX, AND REALLY DON'T KNOW WHAT TO DO ABOUT IT?

THEN THIS IS THE BOOK FOR YOU!

Here, at last, is a battle plan for the defeat of public pornography right in the community in which you live!

Neil Gallagher is a veteran smut-fighter, with an impressive record of successes. For example:

- "The Last Tango" was driven from the screens of a Texas city through his leadership.
- 90% of the stores in one city removed the pornography from their shelves, and all "X" movies left town.
- An airport newsstand, filled with obscene literature one day, was 'clean' the next.

Gallagher has organized campaigns in dozens of American cities, resulting in the elimination of both X-rated movies and Playboy-type pornography.

This book tells you, step-by-step, what you as an individual can do. It details the **Spiritual Strategy**, **Civic Strategy**, and **Legal Strategy**. Obscenity is already illegal in these United States. If you want to know what to do to see the laws enforced, this is your guidebook for effective action.

Bethany Fellowship INC
MINNEAPOLIS, MINNESOTA 55438

PORNO PLAGUE

HOW TO STOP THE

A simple, straightforward action plan that can work in your community.

Neil Gallagher

HOW TO STOP THE PORNO PLAGUE

Comments

You have done a great organizational job in cleaning up smut. I wish we had a Neil Gallagher in every state.

Morton Hill, S.J.
President, Morality in Media
Commissioner, Presidential
Commission on Obscenity
& Pornography

Neil Gallagher and colleagues have won spectacular skirmishes against pornography, but not without wounds. The campaign in this warfare is always vulnerable; but wounds suffered with honor are reflected in scars endured with pride.

Most evident immediately is the social and economic risk by Mr. Gallagher who sacrificed time, income, and personal comfort when he became involved in smut-removal. It is obviously not an exercise for fainthearted, squeamish, or thin-skinned folk.

Edward Hayden, Ed.
The Christian Standard

I have had the privilege of knowing Mr. Gallagher personally and working with him in efforts for decency and of sharing on an inter-faith level with his deep convictions.

I heartily endorse his book for the promotion of human values in the truest Christian sense.

Mother M. Perpetua Hawes
Superioress General
Diocese of San Antonio

Unfortunately, by default, most communities let a minority set the moral standard, but this evangelical mobilized a campaign which succeeded in removing *Playboy* and a number of offensive magazines.

Editorial
Moody Monthly

1F – Ambush on ABC

In *Porn Nation*[26], Oprah calls it "America's #1 addiction."

Right on.

But where were you, oh famous one, when I screamed the same and got assaulted?

They praised you. Slammed me.

Would have liked a little praise back then. Just a little.

That'll help keep me going, I thought.

Turns out there was a Divine Power that eclipsed all human praise. It was that one day in particular…

What it was, they stopped Cal Thomas from going on ABC's *Issues*, fearing he'd quote the Bible.

They didn't stop me.

When it was my turn to appear to discuss my book *The Porno Plague*[27], I tucked my slim New Testament inside my jacket, next to my heart.

I knew something about these gigs. I had made the rounds of university forums, radio/TV shows, newspaper interviews, and churches discussing the healthy and ecstatic view of sex in the Bible as opposed to the dangerous and destructive view of sex in the *Playboy* type magazines and movies.

I liked going to the churches better. Nice to be among friends.

I knew, however, that Jesus went straight to the marketplace, straight to the need. I knew that, ever since *Exodus*, God's messengers from Moses to David and Jesus to Paul invaded enemy territory to conquer and rescue.

---

26 *Porn Nation: Conquering America's Number One Addiction*, Michael Leahy, Northfield Publishing Company, Chicago, Ill, ©2008.

27 Originally, *How to Stop the Porno Plague*, W. Neil Gallagher, Ph.D., (Bethany House Publishers, 1977).

And if there were ever a million-man army to conquer, I was surrounded by it. If there were ever a mission of rescue—to the millions watching—I was put in the front of them, like it or not.

Surrounding me on the set was the ambush: a raging ACLU chief, a pompous professor, a scolding journalist, a mocking host and, this time, the president of C.O.Y.O.T.E.[28] Coiled and ready to spring and strike, they watched the monitor light, eager for it to flip from red to green.

I wasn't there to sever their serpentine heads, and I wasn't there to win an argument. I had taught Symbolic Logic and Metaethics, but I knew these critics weren't here to listen to reason or morality.

This was about facing a million-man army and claiming Asa to do it. Waiting in the green room a moment ago, I had prayed, "This is too big, God. Way too big. Help."

Earlier that morning, on my knees, I said, "God, make my life a miracle of your service."

Always a dangerous prayer.

Feeling sweat on my palms and under my nose, I sat erect under the hot lights illuminating the set and baking the guests. What was I going to say to this mob?

> … [when] you carry my name, you'll be called to testify.
> Make up your minds right now not to worry about it. I'll
> give you the words and wisdom that will reduce all your
> accusers to stammers and stutters.
>
> —Luke 21:12 The Message

---

28 Call Off Your Old Tired Ethics, the Nevada-based organization pushing for national recognition of prostitution.

Does that apply today?

Viewers needed to be told words of truth. It was ugly and sickening, but viewers needed words of truth with love, conviction, and accuracy.

This was the time. This was the place.

Viewers needed to know about NAMBLA, snuff films, Jesus as drag queen, and porn addiction—especially with kids. Viewers needed to know that porn deceived, seduced, and killed. Porn continued to kill families, churches, and nations.

NAMBLA: the North American Man/Boys Love Association where men aggressively practice the seduction of boys and scream for legislation to endorse it.

"Hey, it's the kid's choice," and "If I don't seduce them, someone will."

Lionized in "gay parades" around the country, NAMBLA was becoming a political and public force.

In snuff films, financed and promoted by Mafia types, the victim is "snuffed" out. The victim (called the "star") is snuffed at the end of the film.

She doesn't know that a real murder (hers) will take place in this film.

Snuff films were getting top shelf, and porn magazines were used to seduce models for the snuff films.

Then there were the pictures of Jesus dressed in drag on the covers of *Hustler* and grabbing eyes at neighborhood C stores. There he was: Jesus dressed in a gold sequined gown draped over fishnet hose wrapped around his bloody feet and stuffed into pink stiletto heels.

The caption: "Jesus: Sexy Savior."

And books like *Ministers Lust* proliferated.

Lust, on its cover, showed a grinning preacher shucking his shorts while mounting a teen girl who is spread-eagled on his desk with, of course, her head resting on a Bible. Next to *Lust* is the book *Church Choir Orgy*, detailing what goes on when "they take off their robes and lock the church doors."

The watchdog media were not watching or reporting on these events, although they knew about them. They knew because I showed them. I took the media to the C stores where the *Playboy* sex was displayed next to the gum and candy. I took reporters and police to the adult bookstores where the killer sex was flashed and peddled.

Before I wrote my iconoclastic book, *The Porno Plague*, I had done my homework. And I did my homework each time before I appeared on a TV/radio show or university forum. I knew the cause/effect connection between sex abuse and crime. The police reports were clear and compelling, tragic and terrifying:

- *Attempted Rape—Juvenile Delinquency.* A 15-year-old boy grabbed a 9-year-old girl, dragged her into the brush, and was ripping off her clothes. The girl screamed and the youth fled. The next day he was picked up by police. He admitted that he had done the same thing in Houston, Galveston, and now in San Antonio. He said that his father kept pornographic pictures in his top dresser drawer and that each time he pored over them the urge would overtake him. See Report of Capt. G. E. Matheny, Juv. Off., San Antonio Police.

- *Rape Case.* Woman is raped on the way to church one morning. Just prior to the attack the man was reading obscenity in his panel truck. Cleveland, Ohio. See County Prosecutor Corrigan's story in Universe Bulletin.

- *Rape Case.* Santa Clara County District Attorney Louis Bergna reports, as printed in San Jose, Calif., *Mercury.* "Santa Clara County Crime File documents cases where teenage boys have attacked, and killed, women after their sex drives were ignited by lewd photos from readily available men's magazines. One youth, after seeing a beautiful young girl kidnapped and held prisoner in the British movie, *The Collector*, carted off a girl and held her for18 hours while he forced her to commit every act you can possibly imagine. In his home we found nothing but this type of magazine... The adult bookstores are loaded with books on sadism and masochism—sexual satisfaction through the infliction or receiving of pain." Showing the thin book, the district attorney said it contained photos of women tied up or being beaten up by other women, and it sells for $5.20. "In Santa Clara County we used to think these things were academic," Bergna said, "but a year or so ago police discovered in Sunnyvale a torture chamber where a young professional man beat other men and committed unnatural sex acts. We just completed another case in the Gilroy area in which a young sailor was bound and beaten by another man bent on fulfilling his sexual hunger. *It just might be we have more of this type of thing in this country than we suspect.*"

- *Juvenile Delinquency—Sex Perversion.* Police officer making rounds in city park discovered minor boy committing act of sodomy on another minor boy. Center spread of *Playboy* was being used as means of excitation. See Juvenile Police Officer Frank Meehan, West Covina, Calif.

- *Juvenile Delinquency—Child Molestation.* First Assistant State's Attorney Edward M. Booth, Jacksonville, Fla., writes, "We have four felony charges pending in our criminal courts at this time wherein adults are charged with various sexual offenses involving minor children. In each of these four cases, we have found that obscene literature and other pornographic materials were used to entice minor children ranging in age from 8 to 16 years, including both boys and girls, into indulging in various lewd and lascivious sexual acts with the adults involved... I have found that most cases involving sexual activities with minor children have obscene and pornographic literature and materials involved, and, *perhaps, this is true throughout the country...*"

Five among thousands... all on public record... all censored by the press.

Porn kills.

Just like cocaine or heroin. Hook 'em cheap and easy at first. *Playboy, Penthouse,* and *Hustler.* Then, escalate the addiction to lesbian attacks, snuff films, sex torture, and sadomasochism.

I had listened to counselees tell me how porn had killed their marriages, spouses, and kids. Flashing in my mind was the story of the woman from Western Pennsylvania who, after a conference, grabbed both my shoulders and hugged me. She soaked my lapel with tears. I was the first one she could talk to, she said. I would listen and understand, she pleaded.

Her fourteen-year-old had snatched a porn magazine from a store rack. Boiling with rape, child molesting, and sadomasochism, the magazine urged its readers to seek bigger thrills. Ignited by the magazine's heat, this fourteen-year-old, while masturbating, hanged himself in a barn in rural Pennsylvania.

The ultimate thrill.

After each family conference titled *Morality in America: the Porno Plague,* a stampede of desperate families surrounded me at the back door. Daughters/wives/mothers of deacons and elders and pastors whispering in my ear: "How do I help my father/husband/son? He's hooked."[29]

Porn was killing their marriages, families, and churches.

Christian Parenting Today receives hundreds of letters, emails, or calls like this: "How do I explain to my child that his father's pornography addiction is the primary reason for our marital separation?"[30]

Good question. Let's go to the source of the problem: the pornography itself. Porn kills families because the addicted man wants his wife to look like the brushed up, wildly exaggerated photo of the buxom 19-year-old in the centerfold. Porn kills families because the addicted man (a father, grandfather, uncle, preacher, teacher, business leader, etc.) releases his fired-up lust on that minor girl who looks up to him and trusts him: child, student, employee, etc. Excuses for this incest and molesting:

---

29 The saddest and most sensational example of this leadership addiction was the stunning revelation in 1988 that Jimmy Swaggart was involved with pornographic voyeurism and, ultimately, with a prostitute.

30 Terri Gibbs, Project Manager, *Christianity Today, Women Ask, Women Answer* (Nashville: Thomas Nelson, 2007), 77.

- "If you weren't dressed like that, I wouldn't have gotten excited. It's your fault."

- "You put on that body lotion just so its scent would turn me on. It's your fault for smelling and looking like a little sex doll."

- "The way you fix your hair and brush by me, you look like a 25-year-old and want me to come on to you like a 25-year-old. It's your fault."

It's not her fault. It's never her fault. Not only did she become a victim of incest/molesting, but then she becomes a victim of guilt and pain and shame.

This is the silent scandal in America exploding from the hell of porn: incest and molestation. Even with church leaders. The notoriety surrounding the molesting of young boys and girls within the Catholic church is the tip of the iceberg.

What to do?

If church leaders were sucked in by porn, where's the hope?

Who's speaking the truth? Who's screaming: "The emperor has no clothes!" Who's screaming about the vicious plague of pornography in American society?

- How to recognize it.

- How to run from it.

- How to join with others to stop it.

- How to minister to those who have been abused by it, directly or indirectly.

Who's speaking the truth?

Busting out of my comfortable position as a professor, I spoke and I wrote and I testified. Senate committees, city councils, zoning boards, church assemblies. I told people straight out—and in some cases showed them—what was in the magazines flashing at them beside the bread and milk at their local stores.

Satan's Hell broke loose.

Insults, attacks, lawsuits, threats, ridicule.

Here we go again.

I breathed Asa, adapted to this crisis:

> Help us, O God, for there is none like You
> to help the weak conquer the strong.
> We're here—I'm here—to meet this huge army
> of sex abuse champions.
> I'm here because I trust in You and who You are.
> Don't let these mere mortals stand against You.

Green light on, and the talk-show mob hurled the usual ropes around my neck: "Censorship." "First Amendment rights." "You're a prude." "You must be oversexed yourself." "You don't understand." "You don't have any fun." "Just so long as you don't hurt any other people, it's okay." "You can't legislate morality."

They paused, licking lips and satisfied that the lynching was complete. Surely they snapped my neck and cut my voice box.

I answer with a calm and whisper that stunned me: "Let's talk about sex. What do you think about this? 'A husband's body belongs to his wife. A wife's body belongs to her husband. This empowers both of them to have robust sex any time they want. It makes sex a lifetime permanent party, safe and fun.' Think that's good sexual advice? Overall, do you think it's good sexual advice or not?"

S-l-o-w-l-y, they nodded.

"Know where that's found?"

"Freud," said the prof.

"No."

"Masters and Johnson," said the columnist.

"No."

"Kinsey," said the ACLU guy.

"No."

The talk show host laughed and said, "Yuh, I'm the one who said it."

"Good for you," I joined his banter. "And nice try. Here it is." I slid the New Testament from my pocket, held it before the monitor for millions to see, and read from I Corinthians 7:3-4.

> ³⁻⁴It's good for a man to have a wife, and for a woman to have a husband. Sexual drives are strong, but marriage is strong enough to contain them and provide for a balanced and fulfilling sexual life in a world of sexual disorder. The marriage bed must be a place of mutuality—the husband seeking to satisfy his wife, the wife seeking to satisfy her husband. Marriage is not a place to "stand up for your rights." Marriage is a decision to serve the other, whether in bed or out.
>
> —1 Corinthians 7:3-4 (The Message)

"That's from the Bible, specifically the New Testament, in a book called *Letter to the Corinthians.*" I kept my New Testament opened, propping it on my knee for millions to see the source of truth and love and *the* authority on sex.

"Don't know about you guys," I continued, refusing to yield the mic, "but I've found out that it gives me MORE pleasure to give pleasure to my wife than getting the pleasure myself. She feels the same way. Now that's a party, and that's the way THE authority on sex, God Himself, planned it. Give your life first, then your body. And make a lifetime commitment to please your mate IN EVERY WAY and be loyal to him or her. I know you all agree with that."

Silence.

Except for the whoo! whoo! from the studio audience.

Surprise! Surprise!

They exploded in applause, affirming that people want to be reminded about the beauty and ecstasy of a committed sexual life within marriage. They applauded what they perceived to be a calm, bold, and authoritative speaker. Little did they know that my shirt was soaked from armpit to waist.

The momentum shifted from the stage of ambush to the studio of applause. The host, frozen like a mouse trapped in a corner by hissing cats, cracked the silence with, "Looks like we got a real live one today. Up here <u>AND</u> down there. Let's go to break."

During the break, I thought, "Where did this chutzpah come from to take on a million-man army, to confront and expose leaders of deception and darkness? Seeing the stunned silence of the professor, the press, the prostitute and the host stunned me! What was I doing here playing the game of sound bytes with people whose IQs were below my son's pet lizard?"

My training was in philosophy.

My academic station was to lecture on Kant, Wittgenstein, Whitehead, and Plato to adoring students in ivy-enshrouded classrooms in my native New England. Wasn't that what I was supposed to be doing?

Well, wasn't it?

Wasn't I supposed to be spending my time publishing arcane essays in tame, scholarly journals, rich with polysyllabic words and stunning syllogisms?

What was I doing here?

The answer: GOD PLACES HIS MESSENGERS IN SITUATIONS WHERE GOD WANTS HIS PEOPLE AND WHERE ONLY GOD CAN DELIVER. When Jesus repeated that encouraging statement, "When they drag you into their meeting places or into their courts and before judges, don't worry about defending yourself, what you'll say or how you'll say it," He clearly meant that the right words *will be there.*

"My spirit will give you the right words when the time comes," he was saying: "You don't have to worry about defending yourself. What you say and how you say it, I'll be there. The right words will be there. My Spirit will give you the right words and the right actions when the time comes." (Luke 21:12-15 The Message)

GOD LOOKS *MORE* FOR PEOPLE WITH AVAILABILITY THAN WITH ABILITY. WITH AVAILABILITY—AND ASA—GOD PROVIDES THE ABILITY, AND COURAGE, AND OPPORTUNITY.

I was here because, early and often, I prayed, "God, make my life a miracle of your service…," the compressed version of the Asa prayer.

I saw firsthand that, with Asa power, people were rescued, events were changed, and God got the glory. It had been a wildly unpredictable parade of events. I was thrust in a position of local, then state, then national leadership all done kicking and screaming. And praying.

…still praying when the break is over, and the applause subsides, and the camera returns to me.

I don't wait for an intro.

"Pornography is sex abuse, and sex abuse is slavery, isn't it? It's the slavery of the bodies of women and children and the minds of men. And I know you oppose slavery, don't you?"

Someone mumbled, "Has nothing to do with it."

"I take that to be a *yes*. You oppose slavery, and therefore you oppose the slavery of men, women, and children."

While speaking, I lifted from my pocket a pamphlet I had found on the floor in a dusty corner in an old Boston bookstore, years earlier: *The Negro As Beast: Why Slavery Must Continue*. The book was published in the mid-1800s. I threw it on the table. Might as well have thrown a hissing cobra. Guests gasped and froze.

"Do you guys believe that this book should be published and read and sold? If I understand you right, you guys believe that ANYTHING that ANYONE writes or publishes should be allowed to be circulated and sold."

Silence.

"Silence implies consent. Maybe I didn't make myself clear. You guys believe that anything that anyone wants to write or photograph, they should be able to sell, just like this book *The Negro as Beast*."

The journalist said, "You can't stop people from reading what they want to read."

"Not the point. People can read what they want to read… legally. They cannot sell or circulate whatever they want to sell. They should not have been able to sell this book in the mid-1800s OR ANYTIME, should they? You agree with that, don't you? I asked you a question. They should not have been allowed to sell this book—should they?"

The host smiled and looked at his watch. "Wow... above my pay grade. Let's go to this message, and then we'll let someone else s-m-a-r-t-e-r than me handle that one— Ho... yah!"

I shot: "...And after the break, your answer will be, 'They should NOT have been allowed to sell slavery back then, nor should they be allowed to sell slavery today, which is pornography. Slavery, like *Playboy* porn and its imitators, exploits people and rips them of their dignity.'"

After the break, they slipped in a new guy, the Reverend Cartwright J. Worthington. It's always a setup on these talk shows. TV producers love to use renegade ministers and priests to promote moral anarchy.

Ask Les Brown.

Poor Les.

Brown was groomed to be the male Oprah. Had his own talk show. Didn't last long. Les hated what they were doing because they would ambush HIM, the host. Producers brought on his show religious nuts, transvestites, druggies, pedophiles, and weirdoes of all types. Brown had no idea what they were going to say or do on his show and what lifestyles he was supposed to chuckle at.

"I'm outta here," he announced.[31]

The Reverend Cartwright J. Worthington scolded me: "You cannot legislate morality."

"Wrong," I said. "And I can't believe a smart man like you would drag out that old tired cliché beaten to death by Mayor LaGuardia when he was justifying the sewage of porn in New York decades ago. But since you are a minister, I'm sure you remember the Bible verse, 'Doom to you who legis

---

31 Rush Limbaugh and Ann Coulter told me they no longer give taped interviews. Couldn't agree more. It's always a setup. We learned long ago that, just like the manipulation of Les Brown by his producers, all producers manipulate sound bytes of taped shows to make the show say what THEY want it to say. "All the news that FITS, we print. Or air."

late evil, who make laws that make misery for the poor and rob my people of dignity.' (Isaiah 10:1-2 The Message) Seems to me," I continued, "that if people can legislate immorality, they most certainly can—and do—legislate morality."

"I'd like to see that passage. I'm sure it's out of context."

"You've got me there," I replied. "All I brought with me was my New Testament, but you can look it up. It's in Isaiah 10:1-2. And the good news, my spiritual friend, is the Bible also says that it's the spiritual who judge all things. The spiritual in this case meaning people who believe in rules. Godly, loving, and non-negotiable rules. What you really mean, my good friend, is that *we cannot legislate spirituality.*

We legislate morality all the time.

You cannot make people love what's right, but you can make them do what's right or suffer the consequences. That's what law is for."

"HEAVY, HEAVY, HEAVY. Thanks very much for coming, guys. See you next week." Smiley-Host cuts us off and leaves the set.

Jesus anticipated this reaction when he said:

> I'll give you the words and wisdom that will reduce all your accusers to stammers and stutters.
>
> —Luke 21:15 The Message

When they don't have an answer, they stammer, stutter, or run.

Or slam the teller of truth.

Next day, morning paper called me "the most dangerous man in America." Not just because of the TV debate, but because of the press conference in the airport rotunda. I showed the TV cameras and print reporters what was IN the magazines that they were championing in the name of the First Amendment. I documented for readers and viewers the link between magazine porn and molesting children.

Ironically, the media blasted my ministry as "anti-pornography" and "anti-sex." It wasn't—and isn't—"anti-pornography" or "anti-sex." I am not so much against anything as I am FOR:

- the Biblical view of sex unfolded in the beautiful bonds of marriage,

- the dignity of every individual,

- rescuing slaves and victims.

"Rescuing"... God's mandate for you and me:

> Defend the cause of the weak and fatherless. Maintain the rights of the poor and oppressed. Rescue the weak and needy. Defend them from the hand of the wicked.
>
> —Psalm 82:3-4 NIV

The bombs of hate and criticism in the media, on TV shows, university forums, and newspaper spreads were small, however, compared to the real bombs threatened to be wired to my ignition. They called, and warned me, and hung up. Organized crime, I found out, finances most of the sex shops, sex pulps, and snuff films.

So what.

You claim Asa, you keep going.

My biggest bomb, sadly, came from uninformed Christian leaders—like Nehemiah's detractors taunting him for building a wall and restoring God's city. You discover that when you pierce a dark, evil cellar with a cone of divine yellow light, you expose the rats and they run.

Or bite.

Your heart breaks when you discover that many church folk are into porn,

    ...or mediocrity,

        ...or popularity,

            ...or apathy,

                ...or all four.

I was shattered when seeing that some Christians:

(1) woefully ignored the fact that this was indeed a porn nation and that their own leaders were addicted, and

(2) woefully ignored the fact that Jesus openly rebuked the exploitative and hypocritical as he did with the Pharisees. You know... those guys who attacked Jesus for His embrace of a penitent Mary, who was washing Jesus' feet with her hair. Jesus also rebuked the predatory temple-merchants whose tables He smashed and products he scattered. Jesus was big into public protest, when appropriate.

Max Lucado nailed it: "'I'm angry.'" He didn't have to say it; you could see it in his eyes. Face red. Blood vessels bulging. Fists clenched. 'I ain't taking this no more!' And what had been a temple became a one-sided barroom brawl. What had been a normal day at the market became a one-man riot. And what had been a smile on the face of the Son of God became a scowl. 'Get out of here!' The only thing that flew higher than the tables were the doves flapping their way to freedom. An angry Messiah made his point; don't go making money off people; or God will make hay of you!"[32]

Making money off sex and people: that's porn.

(3) woefully ignored that in the book of Acts, the Apostle Paul used existing laws to promote spiritual ends. (Acts 25:11; Acts 23:13-23; Acts 16:37-40)

Using the law and public protest is a strategy IN CONJUNCTION WITH PRAYER, not in place of.

Some leaders hate your call for action. They want to stay huddled in the warm comforters of <u>personal peace</u> and <u>affluence</u>, as Francis Schaffer put it.

God's people pray for the power to do the impossible. Then they do it. Because it's right. Not for popularity or power.

Hot attacks from some Christians included:

---

32 Max Lucado, *No Wonder They Call Him the Savior* (Nashville: W. Publishing Group, a Division of Thomas Nelson Inc, 1986, 1994) 30.

(a) "Gallagher's a sex addict himself, and this anti-porn war gives him an excuse to look at sex magazines."

(b) "He's Victorian. He resents people who enjoy sex."

(c) "He's running for Congress or mayor or sheriff or dogcatcher—whatever—and he wants the publicity."

(d) "We don't batter our enemies; we just pray for them."

When Asa blasted the sex temples and later conquered the million-man army, he didn't do it because he was hung up on sex and power, or hungry for popularity, or hoped to be "understood" by the brethren. God's people pray for the power to do the impossible. Then they do it. Because it's right and because it rescues.

Porn hurts people. Abortion hurts people. Rape hurts people. Drugs hurt people.

All the academic bromides and spiritual clichés of "whether Christians should slam society's problems" belch from the mouths of ignorant leaders and lethargic church-goers.

Sorry.

The truth is that *any* activity which hurts people is an activity which necessarily grieves Christians, enrages Christians, and inspires us to

pray passionately,

speak boldly, and

act courageously.

Like Asa.

Pray and act.

It's not either/or.

Here's what I tell church leaders: "Are you going to stand on the curb and watch that child get smashed by a speeding truck? You're going to scream at the child to stop. You're going to race into the street to scoop him up. You're going to speak and act to stop someone from being hurt. That IS the Christian life."

When Corrie ten Boom saw Jews being hurt, she did not ponder the propriety of action. She did not engage in theological debates about separation of church and state. She did not muse about, "Jesus is coming back soon, and so we'll just let evil prevail." She acted because she was a compassionate

Christian warrior. She was willing, with God's help, to do the impossible...because she cared with the compassion of a God who invaded the world to rescue hurting people.

Corrie's mandate, like Asa's, like mine—and yours—is to grasp the power of the Asa prayer in one sentence: "God, make my life a miracle of Your service."

And when people say, "How'd you do that?" the answer is, "I didn't. God did it through me. He gets the glory, honor, power, and victory."

No other motive. Some will ask, "Why are you doing this? What are you getting out of this?" I tell them the story of Emerson and Thoreau. Jailed for protesting against unjust laws, Thoreau was asked by Emerson, "Why are you in here?" Thoreau's reply: "Why aren't you?"

The eternal lesson for all believers is: Go ahead and claim Asa for personal growth, spiritual victories, AND public protest, using it to expose sin and crime. You'll learn in a New York second that a battle against evil: abortion, pornography, political correctness, evolution.. whatever... ignites hostility from many in the community and invites suspicion from some in the church.

Sorry about that too.

You learn that calling sin "sin" and crime "crime" does not *cause* separation within a church or community. It illuminates it. The separation, the sin, the compromise is already there. Your holy and compassionate rage reveals it. Like that flashlight in the cellar, the cone of yellow light does not cause the presence of rats. It exposes them.

- Was it worth it?

- Times Square scrubbed.[33]

- Zoning laws passed.

- Bare breast and spread-eagle poses ripped from the front shelves where they had been flashing next to the bread and milk.

---

33 Max Lucado, *No Wonder They Call Him the Savior* (Nashville: W. Publishing Group, a Division of Thomas Nelson Inc, 1986, 1994) 30.

- Child porn laws enacted and enforced.

- Sex merchants driven from many communities.

- And, I pray, many mothers like the shrieking woman in western Pennsylvania are spared future heartaches.

It's been 36 years since my book, *How To Stop the Porno Plague*, was published, and—God bless them—some city leaders still read it and respond to its urgency and relevance:

> "City May Toughen Ordinance on Sexually Oriented Businesses"[34][35]
>
> EULESS, TEXAS: Euless is the latest area city to consider tougher restrictions on sexually oriented businesses. Its proposed law, to be discussed tonight, would effectively ban totally nude dance and impose "no touching" and "no tipping" rules within city limits.
>
> Officials said the proposal wasn't prompted by any new license applications but follows developments in other cities.
>
> Totally nude dancing—not allowed.
>
> Stuffing dollar bills in a stripper's G-string—nope.
>
> Tonight, the Euless City Council will consider tougher licensing requirements for sexually oriented businesses,

---

34 Ironically, many cities cleaned up not for moral or humane reasons, but for economic ones. But they did clean up. In my book, *How To Stop the Porno Plague*, which I sent to thousands of mayors, I documented that when the "porno plague" infects a neighborhood, tenants bolt, tourists flee, crime rockets, property values sink, and reputations are smeared. Those are the reasons ultimately why New York and other cities cleaned up their historic areas. Would that they had done it for Godly and humane reasons… would have been nice.
35 Bryon Okada, "City May Toughen Ordinance on Sexually Oriented Businesses," *Fort Worth Star-Telegram*, March 24, 2009, sec.B-

effectively banning totally nude dances and imposing "no touching" and "no tipping" rules within city limits.

Euless' sexually oriented business ordinance hasn't been amended since 1994, when some of the day-to-day realities of such businesses were not well-defined. Since then, cities across Texas have fought legal battles for control of the businesses, including Arlington and Kennedale.

The Texas City Attorneys Association commissioned a study on the impact that the businesses have on surrounding property values and crime rates. The study, finished in June, showed that off-site sexually oriented businesses have a negative impact on property values. It also shows "that it is a scientific fact sexually-oriented businesses pose large, statistically significant ambient public safety hazards in terms of prostitution, drugs, assault, robbery, and vandalism."

"So what's the relevance," you say. "We *still* have porn."

And we still have poverty.

Jesus said, "…You'll always have the poor among you."

Might also have said, "…You'll always have porn, or gossip, or adultery, or sin among you."

That's why, as God's people, we accept the divine mandate. "Christ in me to do His will and His work."

We whack sin, by prayer and action, wherever and whenever we find it.

Edmund Burke addressed this challenge centuries ago when he said, "The only thing necessary for the triumph of evil is for good people to do nothing."

Good people—God's people practicing Asa—DO SOMETHING. We seize the day to smash sin where we are right now, moment by moment, day by day, and keep going.

OK… And, so what, Gallagher?

"What about me? Is it worth it—and relevant—for me? What's the impact?"

Depends.

Do you accept the commission of Psalm 82:3:4?

> Defend the cause of the weak and fatherless. Maintain the rights of the poor and oppressed. Rescue the weak and needy. Defend them from the hand of the wicked.
>
> —Psalm 82:3-4

Ask Stephanie Voiland if claiming the impossible has impact. For radical obedience. For rescuing people now.[36]

She read Psalm 82:3-4 and prayed, "God, I feel like I'm just going through the motions. Make me radically obedient. Help me to DO THE IMPOSSIBLE FOR YOU." Like Asa, like me, she wasn't sure where those words came from.

She received a quick answer.

> "I got an email that day about a group from our church that was going on a two-week mission trip to Bangkok, Thailand, to work with victims of the sex trade," she says. She'd read about sexual trafficking before that and says the issue broke her heart. "But it seemed like such a big problem, and I didn't think I could do anything about it."
>
> She took the trip, where her group worked with The Well, an organization that provides job training, spiritual guidance, drug rehab, emotional and financial counseling, and even parenting classes.
>
> "We'd start at midnight, in groups of three," Stephanie says. They'd talk to these young hookers who stood outside of bars and cubs, soliciting customers. "We would

---

36 Keri Wyatt Kent, "Not in My Town," *Today's Christian Woman*, November/December 2008: 46-49.

befriend them, tell them about The Well, and that there is an alternative to what they were doing. And we offered to pay their bar fee, which was about $20 U.S. (what they owed 'the house' for their night's work) ."

Their fee paid, the women were free to go, and The Well volunteers offered to take them to a movie or out to coffee. The girls, many of whom were just teenagers, often agreed to go with them.

"They were so surprised we'd be willing to pay to set them free for an evening, even though we didn't know them," Voiland says. "It was really powerful. It gave me a new and profound understanding of redemption. I was struck that God paid so much for me to be free."

Joel Osteen summed it during our "Night of Hope," that historic night at the American Airlines center:

"We ARE the hands and feet of Jesus on Earth."

Whether we feel like it or not… or whether it seems impossible or not… or whether we see results or not.

Joel Osteen and W. Neil Gallagher, Ph.D.

I was blessed to see results, as did Stephanie Voiland. In my case, I received additional blessings. I experienced the same joy as George Mueller did in witnessing the faithfulness of God.

Do you know George Mueller of Bristol?

Talk about divine power to do the impossible daily!

You'll love Mueller.

For 40 years, in his care for thousands of orphans, Mueller raised $8 million through prayer and obedient action alone.

Through the many years of my work, I saw what the Asa prayer and obedient action bring.

Like George Mueller, I had no financial support during those years. But…

- A Christian rancher provided meat.

- A Christian realtor provided a home.

- Hundreds of Christians delivered bags of groceries to our doorstep.

- Others mailed unsolicited checks.

- Medical needs were taken care of by a Christian doctor.

The crescendo of that walk of faith was that long, gray winter weekend when the warmth and light of God's power dramatically became evident. I drove from Memphis to Birmingham in a tiny compact with 235,000 miles on it. The gasket blew, and oil sprayed like Spindletop. I was on the outskirts of Birmingham, and I walked the rest of the way to the sponsoring church for our "How to Stop the Porno Plague" conference.

After the final night of the conference, a pastor approached me and handed me a voucher for a new car to be picked up at a local dealer. During the conference, I had made no appeals for "poor little old me" and a car. (I never appealed for money at any of my conferences.)

For 40 years, Mueller claimed the impossible and watched a mighty God act:

- "Brother T. had 25 shillings in hand and I had three. This enabled us to buy the meat and bread, which was needed; a little tea for one of the houses, and milk for all; no more than this was needed. Now, however, we have come to an extremity. The funds are exhausted…A lady from the neighbourhood of London who brought a parcel with money…and took lodgings next door to the Boys' Orphan-House. This afternoon she herself brought me money, amounting to 3 pounds, 2 schillings. We had been reduced so low as to be on the point of selling those things which could be spared…That the money had been so near the Orphan-House for several days without being given, is a plain proof that it was from the beginning in the heart of God to help us…He allowed us to pray so long; also to try our faith, and to make the answer so much the sweeter. It is indeed a precious deliverance. I burst out into loud praises and thanks the first moment I was alone…I met with my fellow-labourers again this evening for prayer and praise; their hearts were not a little cheered. This money was this evening divided, and will comfortably provide for all that will be needed tomorrow." (p.40)

- "From Yorkshire 50 pounds. Also received One Thousand Pounds today for the Lord's work in China. About this donation it is especially to be noticed that for months it had been my earnest desire to do more than ever for Mission Work in China, and I had already taken steps to carry out this desire, when this donation of One Thousand Pounds came to hand." (p. 65)

- "A gentleman from Manchester stopped at my house. I found that he was a believer who had come on business to Bristol. He had heard about the Orphan-House and expressed his surprise that without any regular system of collections and without personal application to anyone, simply by faith and prayer, I obtained 2,000 pounds and more yearly for the work of the Lord in my hands. This brother, whom I had never seen before, and whose name I did not even known before he came, gave me £2 as an exemplification of what I had stated to him." (p. 88)

Near the end of his ministry, and reflecting on God's provisions, Mueller reminded his readers:

(1) God has not in the least changed since his miracles in the Old Testament.[37]
   - A 92-year-old Sarah gets pregnant.
   - Lot's wife hardens to table salt.
   - Noah builds a boat for an ocean… in the desert.
   - Moses speaks to the sea, and it lays out a dry carpet.
   - The fort of Jericho fizzles.
   - A mad ass speaks up and scolds a prophet.

(2) God's way leads into trial so far as OUR sight and senses are concerned.

(3) This faith is for ALL. "It is the self-same faith that is found in every believer, and the growth of which I have been most sensible of to myself… It has been increasing in me for the last 69 years so long as I continue to practice it."

(4) "I should have been overwhelmed indeed with grief and despair had I looked at things from the outward appearance."

(5) By the grace of God, I do not boast in thus speaking of these victories. I do ascribe it to God alone, that he enabled me to trust in him and has not suffered my confidence in him to fail. [1 Corinthians 15:57-58 NIV]

(6) When you step out in faith, you become more and more acquainted with the nature and character of God and see that God is mighty, wise, and faithful.

(7) Either we trust in God or we trust in ourselves.

---

37 From *Answers to Prayer*, compiled by A.E.C. Brooks from George Mueller's Narratives, Moody Press, Chicago, Illinois, not dated. Used by permission.

And, at age 70, George Mueller was not done yet. He wanted to let the world to know that "GOD LOVES TO DO THE IMPOSSIBLE." He began a career as an evangelist. For the next 20 years, age 70 to age 90, he preached to more than three million people in 42 countries around the world telling of God's power and love and faithfulness.

How did he do it?

Mueller:

> For more than half a century, I have never known one day when I had not more business that I could get through. For 40 years, I have had annually about 30,000 letters, and most of these have passed through my own hands. I have nine assistants always at work corresponding in German, French, English, Danish, Italian, Russian, and other languages.

> But I have always made it a rule never to begin work till I have a good season with God.[38]

He summarized by saying that the most important part of prayer was the 15 minutes AFTER we said, "Amen." "That's when we went to work."

- God loves to do the impossible. Still does.

- He did it through the life of Rick Warren and his book, *The Purpose-Driven Life*, top hardback seller of all time, documenting the power of God's eternal principles. The book received international recognition in the dramatic rescue of fugitive Brian Nichols by Ashley Smith, who used *The Purpose-Driven Life* to help Nichols accept God's grace and mercy and to give himself up.

- God did it through Mother Teresa. The world watched wrinkled hands stroking diseased flesh and responded in awe, because the world longs for God's unconditional love, a love impossible to practice through mere human effort.

---

38 From *Answers to Prayer*, compiled by A.E.C. Brooks from George Mueller's Narratives, Moody Press, Chicago, Illinois, not dated. Used by permission.

- God did it through David Wilkerson. Fifteen-million best-seller *The Cross and the Switchblade*, bestselling film with Pat Boone, and the dynamic growth of Teen Challenge, rescuing youth from drugs and crime.

- God did it through Dr. Ken Cooper.

    Forty years ago, a select few (maybe a few hundred) were jogging and practicing preventative medicine. Today, it's millions.

    Thirty million to be exact, and the person responsible for that "Coopering," as they call it in Brazil, is Christian leader, writer, physician, and champion of preventative medicine, Dr. Ken Cooper, founder of the Cooper Aerobics Center. Dr. Cooper and I shared many radio shows, calling them *Retire Safe, Early, Happy, and Healthy*.

Dr. Kenneth Cooper and wife Millie, Dr. W. Neil Gallagher (center)

Dr. Cooper told our listeners, "Forty years ago, I was a successful flight surgeon in the Air Force with a promising career. I decided to leave, knowing I had a call from God to bring health to the world, a world that was digging its grave with its knife and fork and bags of potato chips and greasy hamburgers and greasier fries. We were as a nation not so much dying on a potato couch, but dying in a fried potato coffin. Fat, lazy, depressed. And the health costs to insurance companies and the government were in the billions. You just know when God's calling you. It's louder than words. I wanted to be a medical missionary, but I didn't realize that God was calling me to be different type of medical missionary."

For the young Dr. Cooper, 40 years ago, it was impossible to launch a medical profession dedicated to preventative health.

It was impossible:

- <u>Professionally</u>. He was criticized and ostracized by the medical community. Doctors were supposed to dispense drugs, give shots, and perform surgeries. Doctors treated disease and injuries. That was their job.
- <u>Financially</u>. "When I left the Air Force to begin my career in preventative medicine and preventative health, Millie was pregnant with our firstborn. I had no money, no support, and no office. In those early months, I prayed fervently and lamented occasionally to Millie, 'Perhaps I should go back in the Air Force. We've got a good career there.' And Millie said, 'Ken, do you really believe that preventative medicine is the wave of the future?' With a certainty that only God could have given me, I said, 'I know it is.'"

  Millie Cooper recalls: "It looked like it was impossible. Many times we came within a hair of declaring bankruptcy. Each Friday, for months, we received a foreclosure notice on the clinic (couldn't meet the bills!). Ken would say, 'I'm going to work. This is what God wants me to do. If the bank hasn't locked the gates, I'm going in, to teach prevention and rescue people early. This is *still* my medical mission.'"

- <u>Physically</u>. "You can't be telling 40-year-old people to get out there and run. There will be dead bodies all over the street in Dallas and everywhere else in the world. You can't tell a man whose had a heart attack and recuperating to ever take out the garbage again, or even take a walk around the block." Physically, I was told… it was impossible to stay healthy the rest of your life.

Prior to Ken Cooper, the medical model was: We find sick and injured people and patch 'em up with drugs and scalpel. That's how doctors make money and build practices. Ken Cooper's medical model is: We find people healthy and early. We pump 'em up with nutrition and exercise. That's how doctors serve God and serve people.

And the serendipity is: On Cooper's model, there are a lot less people who end up sick and injured. And millions more who live longer and healthier lives.

In a three-way discussion with Dr. Cooper, Governor Mike Huckabee, and myself on this topic, Governor Huckabee applauded Dr. Cooper in saying, "What we have in this country is not health insurance. We have disease insurance. Dr. Cooper's model of preventative medicine is truly health insurance and, by the way, saves billions in government and private expenses for insurance and medical care."

Mike Huckabee and Dr. W. Neil Gallagher

Forty years, and 17 books, and 30-million healthy people later, Dr. Cooper testifies to the power of Asa: Claim the impossible and do it.

Claim the impossible task that God has given you!

And do it.

- God did the impossible through... first, a short quiz. What's the third most popular talk show in America?

Answer: "The Doc Gallagher Show on Financial and Family Fitness, of course."

Thanks, but not yet. (We're working on it.) It's the Dave Ramsey Show.. He's a best-selling author and popular talk show host, because he allowed God to do the impossible through him. He has rescued millions from death.

I mean *debt*.

Sound the same, don't they?

And they bring the same pain.

Several hours a day and on hundreds of secular and Christian stations, he teaches God's word about sex, success, marriage, and money.

On *The Dave Ramsey Show: Straight Talk about Life and Money*, Ramsey shatters myths about money and success.

Myth: "Debt is a tool."

Truth: Yeah, a tool for profit for those who issue credit cards.

Myth: "Debt is normal."

Truth: Okay, debt is normal. Be abnormal. Be weird.

Dave Ramsey has an army of listeners who go around bragging, "I m debt-free, and I am weird."

Myth: "Debt is inevitable."

Truth: Only if you want it to be. Start small. Use baby steps. Follow my envelope plan and all the other steps in my book, *The Money Makeover*.

Myth: "If you have a stack of credit cards, it's a sign of prosperity."

Truth: A stack of credit cards is a sign of eventual poverty.

Myth: "We can always catch up later."

Truth: Never presume on the future.

Financial Peace University is the most popular university in America. Open to all who are open-minded.

I've interviewed Dave on my show. I like what he says… particularly on to the message I've been screaming for years: "The greatest compliment you give someone is to hold them responsible for their behavior."

That's where Dave starts. Man up, whether you are a man or a woman, man up. Take responsibility for your behavior.

Here's an example of the thousands of calls that Dave gets every day:

"Dave, we followed your plan, and the first months were the most painful as we went from credit to cash, but we stayed with it, and it's so nice now not to be paying for today and yesterday anymore. By following your plan, we gained peace of mind, we got control of our money, and we stay in focus."

Another: "Dave, because of Financial Peace University, you helped us realize that we had to draw the line and stop living beyond our means. Instead of having to pay our creditors each month, we are finally paying ourselves and investing in our future."

Another: "Dave, establishing my emergency fund was really hard, because I was trying to break my gambling addiction, and money would always get lost. I finally established a budget. The debts became less and less, and now I'm saving for a down payment on a house, and I'll reach my goal next year, thanks to you."

(Another truth that Dave and I enthusiastically agree upon is the issue of gambling and lotteries in places like Choctaw, Bossier City, and Las Vegas. As Dave puts it, "On your way driving to one of those places, just take that roll of hundred-dollar bills and throw it out the window and turn around and head back. That'll save you a lot of time and frustration, because you're going to lose it all, anyway."

Another: "Dave, you helped me to see that that $50 I put on my credit card to pay for dinner and then paid it out with minimum payment would end up costing me, just from minimum payments, $136.32."

The summary of Dave's mission in his own words is this: "With the people who follow *The Total Money Makeover Plan* I have NEVER had anyone write me or call me saying, "I wrote out a budget, I got out of debt, I got on the same page with my spouse, I've built wealth, and I hate it.

No one has ever said that.

Thanks, Dave, for doing the impossible.

- God did it through S. Truett Cathy. Business advisors told him that closing Chick-fil-A on Sundays was insane and impossible.

  Here's how he described it in our interview: "Dr. Gallagher, I made this decision over 50 years ago that I would not be open on Sunday. Everyone told me it was impossible, that Chick-fil-A would not make it if I did that. Restaurants, especially fast-food restaurants, make 20-25 percent of their profits on Sundays. I teach a Bible class for young men. Done it for 50 years. I was not going to miss that, and I was not going to do anything where other people could miss church."

  Fifty years later, and 1,400 restaurants later, and now a dominant force in the highly competitive fast-food industry… God honored Cathy's impossible task. And, by the way, so did Warren Buffett. [39]

39 Truett Cathey, *How Did You Do It, Truett? A Recipe for Success* (Decatur, Georgia: Looking Glass Books, Inc., 2007) [page #?]

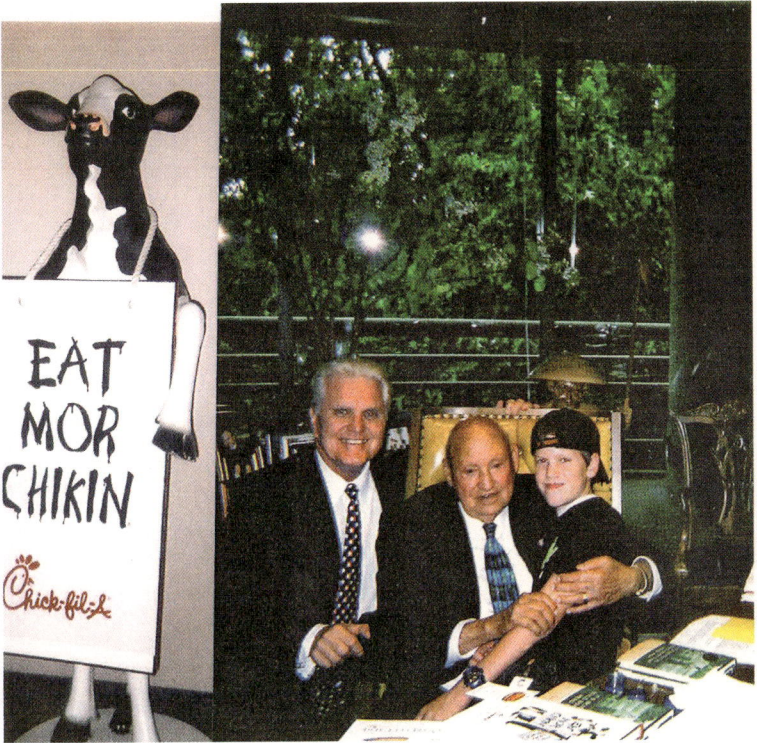

W. Neil Gallagher, Ph.D, Truett Cathy, Founder of Chick-fil-A, and Scotty Gallagher

June 27, 2006

Mr. S. Truett Cathy
Founder and Chairman
Chick-fil-A, Inc.
5200 Buffington Road
Atlanta, GA 30349-2998

Dear Truett:

I enjoyed both your letter and the annual report. I particularly liked your comments about being 85 with a lot of good years ahead. You and I have the same philosophy toward life.

With the fun you are having with your business, you are 100% right in not selling it. How could the world be any better?

Your offer of a Chick-fil-A sandwich is powerful – particularly with the added salt thrown in. Keep a seat reserved for me at your lunch table.

Truett, I really admire what you've accomplished. And with you at the helm, the best is yet to come.

Best regards.

Sincerely,

Warren E. Buffett

WEB/db

God called all these, like Asa, to action. He didn't call them to inform or entertain.

Les Stobbe, editor-in-chief of the Christian Writers Guild said, "What I see in far too many Christian programs and books is an entertaining, informative presentation that settles for barely a hint at action to be taken."[40]

Mueller, Cooper, Ramsey, and Cathy—each had a goal not merely to inform or to entertain, but to act—to do the impossible empowered by an unstoppable God, and in doing so, they have inspired millions to do the same.

GOD LOVES TO DO THE IMPOSSIBLE.

Remember the song that says: "And here is the best part: You have a head start if you are among the very young at heart." Well, this is the best part.

Ready?

Really ready?

Box of Puffs nearby, brushing the side of your wrist?

- God not only loves to do the impossible, but He's proven it:
- God in a diaper in a dirty barn. For us.
- God letting barbed wire rake across his back. For us.
- God accepting gobs of smelly spit pelting his face. For us.
- God taking sucker punches while stumbling up a hill. For us.
- God dangling like a bloody scarecrow on skin-shredded wrists, punctured with half-dollar sized holes. For us.
- God bouncing out of the cave of death. For us.

Didn't do it for fame, or power, or bragging, or money. Did it for us: folks with smelly armpits and headaches, pimples and worries, stubby chins and menstrual cramps, tempers and moods.

God's got skin in the game. Still does the impossible.

God's people...

    praying the Asa prayer,

        fulfilling God's purposes,

            using God's plans,

                to achieve the impossible.

What million-man army are you going to take on today?

---

40 Les Stobbe, "Enlisting Your Reader for Life Change" *Christian Communicator Magazine* November/December 2008, 5.

Say it.. go ahead and say it… "God, make my life a miracle of your service."

And watch in awe and wonder as God gets the glory of your "impossible" actions.

Like turning rejection into rewards, and betrayal into a blessing.

You'll see…

* * * * * * * * *

1G – The Betrayal

1G – The Betrayal

Tony Robbins, Suze Orman, and I have much in common. And I don't mean books, DVDs, and gigs.

Done that.

We've also been sacked and smacked. We've had the thrill of returning to our offices and finding we've have been robbed or sabotaged.

You can look it up.

It's in Tony and Suze's books and tapes.

Tony tells how a trusted business partner embezzled $750,000. Suze tells of returning to her office one Monday morning to find her files gone and desk savaged—by a trusted business partner. Worse, in Suze's case, partner-turned-competitor trashed Suze's name.

That was *my* million-man army.

Et tu, Brute?

Who said that? Caesar to Brutus?

Yes.

And me to Big Al.

Razor ripped across my Adam's apple. Thanks a lot, Albert.

Background:

After years dedicated to the "anti-pornography" work and training thousands of leaders, I gladly yielded the leadership of that work to the two organizations better equipped (and staffed fulltime) to expand and promote that important work: Focus on the Family and The American Family Association. I returned to fulltime writing and motivational workshops.

A New York brokerage firm approached me and offered me a position as financial counselor/broker. ("You have great communication skills.") I built a successful career with Big Broker. My job, first with Big Broker in New York and then with Big Broker in St. Louis, was this: "Put on your headset and dial a hundred suckers a day."

Only they didn't call them suckers.

Dial a hundred people a day, and you'll find one a day who is naïve, impulsive, or greedy enough to send $10,000, $100,000, $250,000, even $500,000. Over the phone. Yeah, they're out there.

Are they EVER out there! That's how Bernie Madoff and others like him were able to rip off thousands. Never have understood how the Bernie Madoffs of the world prosper.

Personally, I do not accept an account from a client unless we've had a face-to-face meeting. Several of them. Don't care how warm the referral is or how eager they are to say they want to invest with me. Never will I open up an account unless we've had a face-to-face meeting, and I recommend to all advisors and clients reading this that they adopt the same practice.

I became uncomfortable with this demand that I "smile and dial" for profits. Business, it seemed to me, is primarily about people, not about profits. I prayed Asa about this "impossible" mission of putting people before profits.

And I saw that it comes down to this: Can you succeed on Wall Street by putting people above profits? That's the divine question. And the answer came in the form of a question. I realized there was only one question a client should ask in a financial transaction, and it is this. "Mr. CPA, Lawyer, Stock Broker, CFP, Senior Advisor, whatever he or she calls himself, Mr. or Ms. Financial Person… IF I DIDN'T HAVE ANY MONEY WITH YOU, WOULD YOU STILL CARE ABOUT ME?"

It's an extension of Zig Ziglar's motto, "You can get anything in life you want if you just help enough other people get what they want." What they want. Others first.

Business world now promotes this approach—calling it spirituality—because they say it, well, works.

Hul-loo…

Doctor Tony Allesandra:

Spirituality is the bond of trust that you're able to create with others, the level of caring and the attitude of service that you convey, and the sense of higher purpose or greater good that you communicate…

There is evidence that these kinds of spiritual issues are becoming more important in all areas of our national life: in business, in healthcare, and even in how we see relationships between family and friends.

(No kidding??!! WNG)

An article in Business Week estimates that more than 10,000 Bible and prayer groups meet regularly in workplaces. The number of new books each year connecting spirituality with career and success has quadrupled since 1990... There are many reasons why all this is happening... Connecting with people on a spiritual level just plain works.[41]

Big Broker in New York and Big Broker in St. Louis ignited in fury, back then, when I practiced spirituality. (What's to practice? If you've got Him, you'll give Him in loving service. If you ain't got Him, there's nothing to give. It's as normal as breathing.) Anyway, Big Broker asked: Why would I instruct clients to ask such a "stupid question"? *(If I didn't have any money with you, would you still care about me.)*

First, Big Broker didn't understand the question. Second, that's not the model of the brokerage business. Big Broker's model is a restaurant: Keep the door swinging and the booths full. That's how you make money. Thus, when I spent two hours talking to a client about their grief, their goals, their family... and they left without buying Big Broker's mutual fund, variable annuity, stock, or bond, I was scolded. Ripped.

Fortunately, I listened to my wife.

Ah, the wisdom of a thoughtful, supportive spouse. "Honey, you're the financial speaker for Zig Ziglar's *Born to Win* conferences, you earned an Ivy League doctorate, you're a counselor, you're a writer. Just educate. Forget about this cold call stuff and meeting Big Broker's demands and quotas."

I left Big Broker and opened an independent counseling office. I taught and I lectured: hospitals, schools, colleges, churches, lawns, parks, synagogues, cafeterias... wherever I could get a hearing. I built a successful career as an independent investment educator, focusing on estate and

---

41 Tony Alessandra, *The 10 Qualities of Charismatic People* Audio CD (Niles, IL: Nightingale-Conant Corporation 2000).

financial planning. I decided, early on, to build my practice on the service model of the Billy Graham Evangelistic Association (BGEA).

Graham combines a fervent belief in his own calling with the idea that he personally deserves none of it. As a result, he tries to bring together people who share his mission and lets them have their say.

"Because he never took his eyes off the long-term goal [of preaching the gospel], he had lots of ideas about how to get there, but he was willing to listen to reason when they didn't make sense."

"Often people tend to define leadership as being like an orchestra conductor," said Larry Ross, who has managed Graham's media relations for 28 years. "But the model for Graham would be a jazz band leader. He taps his foot, keeping the tone, setting the direction…"[42]

The direction for us, GFG, Inc.,[43] is summed in our mission statement. You will see it when you enter our lobby. You'll see it on our literature. "OUR MISSION IS TO BE A VEHICLE OF GOD'S PEACE AND COMFORT TO AS MANY PEOPLE AS POSSIBLE, HELPING FIRST WITH THEIR FINANCIAL PEACE OF MIND AND ALSO WITH THEIR SPIRITUAL, EMOTIONAL, AND FAMILY WELLBEING."

That vision acknowledges that financial success is only twenty percent about money. Financial success incorporates all dimensions of human personality: spiritual, emotional, family, financial, and physical.

Daily, as financial professionals, we face the battle of greed.

Nothing wrong with profit… but greed's different. Greed is to profit as lust is to sex. Profit and sex are healthy forces of energy. When internalized to personal power only, they become greed and lust.

Daily I prayed Asa:

LORD, there is no one like You

---

42 Amy Reeves, "Billy Graham's Higher Calling." *Investor's Business Daily*, July 6, 2009, page 4
43 Gallagher Financial Group, Inc.

to help the powerless against the mighty.
Help us, LORD our God,
     for we rely on You,
and in Your Name
     we have come against this vast army.
LORD, You are our God;
     do not let mere mortals
     prevail against You.

Did well, thank you, Lord, helping eleven thousand clients with nearly one billion dollars.

And growing.

At one point, I added Albert—Big Al—to my team.

One day, Big Al suffered a mild heart attack. Gave him time off. Lots of time. With pay, no questions asked.

No legal requirement on my part to do it. Just seemed like the right thing to do. I wanted to help the guy. I appreciated him and trusted him and told him so.

He returned to work and wanted to build a little real estate business of his own. No problem. Go ahead and use Gallagher Financial phones, computers, and copy machines, and I'll use my radio show and books and television appearances to promote your business. I don't want a dime.

Come to find out, he was setting me up and stealing files, records, and passwords. He assumed I was an amiable dunce, inept and naïve.

What kind of a business leader—especially in the competitive area of financial services—puts his employees' needs above his own? What kind of a boss gives an employee weeks off, with pay, no questions asked? Big Al had seen me do it for other employees as well.

"What a dummy Doc is."

So… conspiring with three others, he orchestrated plans to open his own office, steal my database, and torch my business and reputation.

Caught him and fired him.

Too late.

Somehow he slithered in, grabbed hundreds of files, trashed my computers, and called clients to tell them the Big Lie: "I couldn't stand Doc's business practices anymore, and so I decided to quit… and would you like to transfer your account to me?"

Razor went from Adam's apple to aorta: He called state regulators to "report" me for alleged and false violations. (Smart move: that'll tie you up for months, if not years.)

Regulators, I discovered, love to hear from disgruntled employees. They've got scripts ready for these malcontents to recite, thereby dumping revenge on their former bosses.

Thousands of dollars in legal bills to produce records and defend my innocence against Big Al's charges. ("Defend my innocence?" For <u>what</u>? I didn't do anything.)

Doesn't matter. With some crusading regulators, the attitude is, "Don't confuse me with the facts." If they can't find a bad guy, they'll create one.

Remember the travesty with the Duke University students and the crusading attorney, Nifong? In that case, crusader turned out to be criminal. Nifong, in his zeal, suppressed exculpatory evidence and manufactured condemnatory evidence. Mercifully for the Duke students and their families, Nifong got caught, lost his law license, and was thrown in the slammer.

That regulator got deregulated, defrocked, and detained behind bars.

John Grisham documented the systemic abuse of power-hungry regulators (and the people victimized by it) in his book *The Innocent Man*.[44]

My victory wasn't as clean and easy. I found out that the rules of evidence in the hands of some regulators are fluid and arbitrary. I found out that judges and juries are unpredictable and subjective.

"I'm going to be wiped out," I thought. "This is too big an assault. God, this is W-A-Y too big. This IS a million-man army, and I feel helpless."

I prayed Asa loud and often.

---

44 See *DeLorean* (Ted Schwarz, *DeLorean* (Grand Rapids: Zondervan Publishing House, 1985)) for an even more outrageous example of how regulators manufacture—or suppress—evidence to promote their ends, including the total destruction of their target victims. Regulators especially love it when the target is high profile documented in John Grisham's *The Innocent Man* (New York: Bantam Dell Pub Group,2006) and Randall Adams's *Adams V. Texas:* Adams, Randall , William Hoffer, and Marilyn Mona Hoffer, (New York: St. Martin's Press, 1992).

And I felt like Schuller's dad returning to their ravaged farm after that famous tornado: "*It's all gone, Jennie. Jennie, it's all gone. Twenty-six years, Jennie, and it's all gone in ten minutes.* Dad got out of the car, ordering us to wait, and walked with his cane around the clean-swept tornado-vacuumed yard. We later found out that our house had been dropped in one smashed piece a half mile out in the pasture. We had a little sign on the kitchen wall, a little plaster motto: 'Keep looking to Jesus.' It was God's message to Dad. *Keep looking to Jesus.*"[45]

How do I go home and tell my wife the business was smashed and gone? Years of struggles, thousands of appointments, and a hundred thousand disappointments, delays, or rejections. Millions of risk capital put to work to build a premier consulting business. Thousands of clients who needed and trusted me.

Was it gone? Was it really, really all gone?

I wanted to melt in despair.

Or smash Big Al's face in hate and fury.

I screamed with rage and cried out in panic.

I shuffled to bed at night and woke each morning feeling a hundred-pound bag of cement on my chest. My blood thickened to mud and my brain to glue. There were days when I couldn't move and I couldn't think.

David spoke to my despair:

> Hostile accusers appear out of nowhere. They stand up and badger me.

> When I was down they threw a party. All the nameless riffraff of the town came chanting insults about me. Like barbarians desecrating a shrine, they destroyed my reputation. God, how long are you going to stand there and do nothing?

> —Psalm 35:11-17 The Message

---

45 Robert H. Schuller, *Tough Times Never Last, but Tough People Do!*, (Nashville: Thomas Nelson, Inc., 1983.

God loves to do the impossible. God loves to do the impossible. I made myself say those words taped to my bathroom mirror:

> LORD, there is no one like You
>> to help the powerless against the mighty.
>
> Help us, LORD our God,
>> for we rely on You,
>
> and in Your Name
>> we have come against this vast army.
>
> LORD, You are our God;
>> do not let mere mortals
>>
>> prevail against You.

Long story (a very long story) short and, inch by inch, God honored my Asa prayer, and I rebuilt my career. Step by step, moment-by-moment, I acted on the promise and power of Asa.

I was exonerated from Big Al's accusations. I rebuilt my business… bigger and better.

To the point where I received a proclamation from the governor thanking me and my company for our compassionate and practical work helping investors, particularly seniors. Only financial firm in Texas to receive such a proclamation.

I wrote the popular *The Money Doctor's Guide to Taking Care of Yourself When No One Else Will*.[46] I am now a columnist for *Bottom Line*, a national consumer bulletin. I am featured with Jack Canfield (of *Chicken Soup* fame) on the CD series, *Strategies for Excellence*. I am the financial speaker for the Zig Ziglar *Born to Win* seminars, and our practice is flourishing.

The serendipity of this for clients and me is that in 2008, when 40 million Americans lost 50 percent or more in their brokerage accounts, 401Ks, retirement plans… our clients lost nothing.

You read that right. Nothing. That's divine IMPACT. Our business is flourishing and strong.

---

[46] W. Neil Gallagher, Ph.D., *The Money Doctor's Guide to Taking Care of Yourself When No One Else Will*, (New York: John Wiley & Sons, 2004).

Remember the headlines? "Stocks Off $2.1 Trillion This year: Biggest June Loss Since the Great Depression," "For Many Today, Golden Years Means Less Travel, More Work," "Struggling to Pay the Bills," "The New Depression." And then there were the thousands who lost their thousands to the scammers, like Bernie Madoff.

Not us, not our clients.

During this turbulence, our clients were safe and their portfolios solid.

Out of the inferno of trial and persecution, which Big Al ignited, God empowered us to build a sleep-at-night practice, a fortress for our clients.

We use three strategies for financial success. I call it the WIN strategy, the same strategy I recommended to Dave Ramsey:

W = Wisdom—We ask for wisdom to discern what's best for our clients.

I = Independent—We're independent, not captive to any bank, brokerage firm, or insurance company.

N = No risk.

God loves to do the impossible: Even with helping His people with money. Maybe especially helping people with His money. HE WANTS HIS PEOPLE TO ENJOY—ENJOY— THE IMPOSSIBLE: REMAIN STRONG AND PROFITABLE WHEN EVERYONE ELSE IS SCARED AND PANICKY.

Big Al? Did you forgive him?

Are you crazy? How could I?

Nearly killed my family and my career.

Forgiving Big Al would be a billion-man army, not a mere million-man.

But what about Corrie?

That thought hit me like a hammer-blow to my forehead. Corrie **did the impossible and forgave** her Nazi tormentors:

> It was a church service in Munich that I saw him, the former S.S. man who had stood guard at the shower room door in the processing center at Ravensbrück. He was the first of our actual jailers that I had seen since that time.

And suddenly it was all there—the roomful of mocking men, the heaps of clothing, Betsie's pain-blanched face.

He came up to me as the church was emptying, beaming and bowing. "How grateful I am for your message, Fräulein," he said. "To think that, as you say, He has washed my sins away!"

His hand was thrust out to shake mine. And I, who had preached so often to the people in Bloemendaal the need to forgive, kept my hand at my side.

Even as the angry, vengeful thoughts boiled through me, I saw the sin of them. Jesus Christ had died for this man; was I going to ask for more? *Lord Jesus,* I prayed, *forgive me and help me to forgive him.*

I tried to smile. I struggled to raise my hand. It was impossible. I felt nothing, not the slightest spark of warmth or charity. And so again I breathed a silent prayer. *Jesus, I cannot forgive him. Give Your forgiveness.*

As I took his hand the most incredible thing happened. From my shoulder along my arm and through my hand, a current seemed to pass from me to him, while into my heart sprang a love for this stranger that almost overwhelmed me.

And so I discovered that it is not on our forgiveness any more than on our goodness that the world's healing hinges, but on His. [47]

I prayed Asa again, sank to my knees, and prayed forgiveness and grace over Big Al, repenting of my hardness and admitting, like Corrie, that it's through God's forgiveness in us that all relationships are healed.

* * * * * * * * *

Time out! Gallagher, I don't identify with this.
None of this. Not reading anymore.

---

47 Ten Boom, Corrie, *The Hiding Place* (Peabody: Hendrickson Publishers, 2009) 261-262.

I've never led a crusade against sin and crime. I've never owned a business or been betrayed. I've never been called upon to forgive somebody who tried to kill me and my family.

But you have gone to bed at night hoping you wouldn't wake up. You've had that experience that King David confessed when he said, "I'm tired of all this, so tired. My bed has been floating 40 days and nights in the flood of my tears. My mattress is soaked, soggy with tears. The sockets of my eyes are black holes, nearly blind. I squint and I grope." (Psalm 6:6-7 The Message) You have been so depressed that your speech was slush and your knees were napkins. What you forgot—and I almost forgot—was that GOD LOVES TO DO THE IMPOSSIBLE. The claim and victory of Asa was true then. And true now.

With Asa, you can even take on a raging atheist…

＊ ＊ ＊ ＊ ＊ ＊ ＊ ＊

Greetings:

As Governor of Texas, I am pleased to extend greetings to all in attendance at the annual North Texas Expo on Aging *Celebrating Life* 2008.

Senior Texans have cared for families and communities, enhanced economic prosperity, defended our country, and preserved and protected the vision of our founding fathers. Through time, they have shared life's experiences and expertise, paving paths of progress, defining the foundation of which we continue to further the successes of today. They have built a legacy of excellence that will long endure.

I am certain that this expo will offer a wealth of lessons to our seniors, their adult children and caregivers, and others on financial literacy, health and best of all, *"How to live for tomorrow."* I commend the *Mature Texan Magazine*, The Gallagher Group and AARP in your efforts and commitment to serve senior Texans. You highlight the best of the Lone Star State.

First Lady Anita Perry joins me in extending our best wishes for the future.

Sincerely,

Rick Perry

Rick Perry
Governor

Dr. Neil Gallagher
Gallagher Financial Group
1845 Precinct Line Road Suite 215
Hurst, TX 76054

Dear Doc:

Thanks for the great job you did at our Born To Win Seminar. Each of our 192
participants benefited from your powerful message! You really did "knock 'em
alive!"

The financial information and insights you share are right on target. Your "Retire Safe,
Early and Happy" message has meaning for a wide range of people. It is well
prepared, well researched, well presented and well received. Your approach to a
balanced financial plan is in perfect alignment with our goal setting formula. Several
participants commented on the ease of following and implementing this formula.

Doc, you always enjoy presenting this talk and our participants always enjoy hearing it.
Your platform skills were excellent and your use of humor to involve the audience was
very effective.

Once again, thanks for a great presentation.

Sincerely,

Zig Ziglar

50 Million Americans Approach Retirement Sick, Broke, Scared or Alone! Will You Be One of Them?

It's a subject too many of us don't want to address. No one wants to think about getting old. It's an unpleasant thought to many, but according to W. Neil Gallagher, Ph.D. it's imperative that you do – and now. He says it's the difference between retiring "sad, mad and poor" and "safe, early, and happy".

America is in the midst of a health care crisis... and most Americans are right in the thick of it. They're in the unenviable position of being responsible for both the care giving of their aging parents and their own children. This is a daunting task both financially and spiritually that no other generation has ever had to deal with. Imagine the stress of paying for your parent's nursing home, your children's college education, and your mortgage! Top that off with the hard fact that you've also got to start planning for your own old age and retirement security.

W. Neil Gallagher, Ph.D., can help. Known as "The Money Doctor", he has made a career out of helping people plan for their financial future.

Dr. Gallagher will reveal:
- Why you can't depend on the government to take care of you.
- How to ensure that you and your loved ones are protected.
- Why it's never too early to start planning retirement for yourself and your loved ones.

*** W. Neil Gallagher, Ph.D., has been providing financial planning services for two decades and hosts the financial talk show, "The Money Doctor". He is a former university professor and author of the book, THE MONEY DOCTOR'S GUIDE TO TAKING CARE OF YOURSELF WHEN NO ONE ELSE WILL and co-presenter of the new DVD, SUCCESS STRATEGIES with Jack Canfield ("Chicken Soup" creator). His articles have appeared in Senior Market Advisor and The Journal of Value Inquiry. Dr. Gallagher has been interviewed on hundreds of radio stations as well as ISSUES, THE 700 CLUB and The ABC Nightly Report.

*** THE MONEY DOCTOR'S GUIDE, published by John Wiley & Sons, is available at Barnes & Noble and Amazon.com

AVAILABILITY: Texas, nationwide by arrangement and via telephone.
CONTACT: Rosie Escobar at 1-800-434-4362 or visit our web site at www.docgallagher.com

"Doc... Thanks for your help. You're the best!"
      -Frank Lucchesi, Former Manager, Texas Rangers

"We loved your presentation to our company... We want you back!"
      -Zig Ziglar

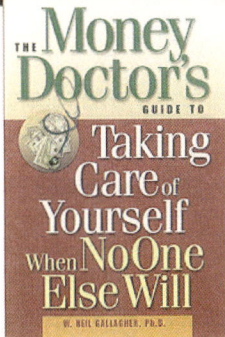

A JAMES WASLASKI PRODUCTION

SUCCESS STRATEGIES

QUEST for EXCELLENCE
INTERVIEW SERIES

POWERFUL...SPIRITUAL...ENLIGHTENING

A BLUEPRINT FOR LIFE AND BUSINESS SUCCESS

ORTHOPEDIC MASSAGE & PAIN MANAGEMENT

Doc Gallagher
Financial Journalist,
Author, Speaker

Aaron Mattes
Kinesitherapist, Author,
International Lecturer

Jeff & Linda Riach
Entrepreneurs,
Owners of Osteowista, Inc.

Jack Canfield
Founder and Co-Creator
Chicken Soup for the Soul

Nance Guilmartin
Emmy Award
Winning Author

George Kousaleos
Founder, Owner
The CORE Institute

Nick & Maggie
Brooks-Carter
Osteopathic Entrepreneurs

Perry Isenberg
Vice-President
Performance Health

Validea's top "Lynch picks" now…

Apollo Investment Corp. (AINV) is a closed-end investment company that invests in the stock and debt of other companies. With more than $1 billion in assets under management, the company has experienced rapid earnings growth in recent years. *Recent share price:* $22.54.

Exxon Mobil Corp. (XOM), the huge oil and gas company, is trading at an attractive price relative to its earnings growth. *Recent share price:* $75.50.

POSCO (PKX), a Korean steel producer with $27 billion in annual sales, recently traded at a P/E barely above 5. *Recent share price:* $78.84.

VALIDEA HOT LIST

Which stocks would history's greatest investors pick today if they collaborated on their investment decisions? Validea's Hot List tries to answer this question by bringing together the stock-screening processes of 10 Wall Street legends—Warren Buffett, David Dreman, Ken Fisher, Benjamin Graham, Peter Lynch, John Neff, William O'Neil, James O'Shaughnessy, Joseph Piotroski and Martin Zweig. The resulting Validea Hot List portfolio has produced an average annual return of 36% since its inception in July 2003, compared with a return of 10.4% for the S&P 500.

Today's leading Hot List picks…

IndyMac Bancorp, Inc. (NDE) is a mortgage originator whose stock offers a 4.5% yield. It is a quality company that has a history of strong earnings growth. *Recent share price:* $43.98.

Telefonos de Venezuela (VNT) is a Venezuelan telecom company. Any investment in volatile Venezuela is risky, but this stock's tiny P/E of 7, huge dividend yield of 11.6% and minuscule debt-to-equity ratio of 0.02 suggest that it might be a reasonable risk to take. *Recent share price:* $19.58.

Thor Industries, Inc. (THO), a leading manufacturer of recreational vehicles and buses, has a 10-year record of predictable earnings growth, a debt-to-equity ratio of zero and a reasonable P/E of just 14. *Recent share price:* $44.62. ■ ■

W. Neil Gallagher, PhD ■ The Gallagher Group

How to Be Certain Your Retirement Money Won't Run Out

Most people don't mind the idea of having to work a few years past retirement age or cutting back a bit on spending, but many of us are afraid of someday running out of money in retirement.

Whether you are retired, approaching retirement or concerned about your elderly parents, there are steps you can take to ensure financial security.

LONG-TERM-CARE INSURANCE

Start coverage when you are in your 40s or 50s if you can afford it. You are more likely to be in good health than in later years, which means your rates will be low. It still pays to buy long-term-care (LTC) insurance even if you're in your 60s or 70s, but you might be able to afford only a bare-bones policy. *Sample cost:* A 45-year-old man can get a policy with a $300 daily benefit (the average daily cost for nursing homes in my area of Texas) for a benefit period of 10 years for less than $100 a month in premiums.

Ask whether your employer will purchase a policy on your behalf, or check whether LTC insurance is included in your company's "cafeteria" plan. Business owners are permitted by law to pay the premiums for an employee and his/her spouse. Many firms now offer this as a perk to attract or retain valued employees. *Careful:* If your employer purchases your LTC policy, you'll have to pay tax on the benefits. However, the money you save on premium payments may still make this desirable. Also, many company policies are not "portable," so it may be preferable to own your own individual policy in the

event that you leave the company.

What to look for in an LTC policy…

Benefit period of at least three years. The benefit period is the amount of time the insurer contractually promises to cover your nursing home or home-care expenses. I prefer at least a three-year period because the average nursing home stay is about 2.5 years.

Daily benefit amount that is 100% of the prevailing nursing home cost in your area. To find out that cost, contact your state's Department of Aging or ask LTC insurance providers.

Home health-care coverage. Make sure that benefits will be paid even if you don't need to enter a nursing home but do need at-home care.

Inflation protection. Your premiums stay level, but your daily benefit typically increases by 5% a year.

For information on LTC policies, contact your state's Office of Insurance Commissioner or Department of Insurance. You can find a link to your state's Department of Insurance at the National Association of Insurance Commissioners Web site (www.naic.org, click on "NAIC States & Jurisdictions").

EQUITY-INDEXED ANNUITY

It is wise to keep a portion of your money in stocks even if you are re- ▶

Bottom Line/Personal interviewed W. Neil Gallagher, PhD, founder and CEO of The Gallagher Group, a financial-planning firm in Dallas.

He is a certified elder-planning specialist and author of *The Money Doctor's Guide to Taking Care of Yourself When No One Else Will* (Wiley). www.docgallagher.com

25 best services, companies & organizations for seniors!

Hat's off to all these fine companies that have made the "L" List! These companies & organizations have shown strong leadership through their services, customer service & community outreach.

Congratulations to each of you and keep up the great work.

Way to be the BEST!

Dr. Gallagher, "America's Money Doctor," is a graduate of Brown University (Ph.D.) and former professor of Texas Christian University. Author of 38 professional and popular articles, he is an independent investment educator with expertise in:

- Wealth preservation
- Income enhancement
- Tax-protection, and
- Estate planning.

He has appeared on several radio and television shows including (locally) KDXM-TV, WRR, KRLD, KLTY, and KAAM where he currently hosts the "Your Family Matters" show.

He is on the faculty of Zig Ziglar's "Born to Win" seminars, and has spoken to many professional, business, and service groups including employees/retirees of American Airlines, Southwestern Bell, Hitachi Corporation, Lockheed Martin, Bell Helicopter, AT&T, and Alcatel. He has also spoken to hundreds of church, educational, civic, and service groups.

Dr. Gallagher's latest book, *The Money Doctor's Guide to Taking Care of Yourself When No One Else Will*, has helped thousands of readers to enjoy a healthy financial future.

One of the contributions Doc Gallagher has given 25 ladies in Texas is an annual day of glory by presenting the Ms. Texas Senior Pageant. Doc Gallagher is an incredible role model for businesses, leaders, and team members, and has always shown his loyalty to the 50-plus demographic community since day one.

28 | www.mature texan.com

Active Retirement Living
Highland Spring Community - Dallas, Texas
Village of Stone Brooke - McKinney, Texas
Juliette Fowler Homes - Dallas, Texas

Home Health Care Providers
medical & non-medical
Care Improvement Plus - Fort Worth, Texas
Home Care Network of Texas
Maxim Health Care of Texas
Professional Caretakers, Inc - Fort Worth, Texas

Resources for Seniors
Senior Citizens Services - Fort Worth, Texas
Area Agency on Aging - The State of Texas
Senior News Source - Dallas, Texas
Sheltering Arms - Houston, Texas

Financial Resources for Seniors
The Gallagher Group - Dallas, Texas
800-43-44-DOC
docgallagher.com

Medical & Mobility Services
Wright - Way, Inc - Dallas, Texas
The Scooter Store - New Braunfels, Texas

Continued Care / Assisted Living
Autumn Leaves Memory Care In Texas

Hospice Care
Hospice Austin - Austin, Texas
The Comfort Home - Mc Allen, Texas

Organization for Senior 's
Ms. Texas Senior America Pageant
Gold Medallion Club - Bryan, Texas

Geriatric Care Management
Senior Life Line - Grapevine, Texas
Sheltering Arms - Houston, Texas

Skilled Nursing &Rehabilitation Centers
The Concierge - Houston, Texas

1H - The Atheist Debate

1H – The Atheist Debate: Colorado High

I tapped the chemistry professor on his shoulder while he scratched on the board with cigar-thick chalk. A cloud of white dust rose from the crumbling chalk, blanketed the back of his hand like powdered sugar, and floated to my nostrils.

"Sir, do you mind if I—"

"Don't talk to me now," he snapped. "If I don't answer your question during class, you make an appointment to see me later."

"Sir, I'm not here—I'm not one of your students. I'm not up here to ask you a chemistry question. We have a debate in this room right after class. Do you mind if I make the announcement?"

"Go ahead," he barked, his voice bouncing off the ancient green board, while I stared at the back of his head.

I turned and faced the 500 students in the University of Colorado Chemistry Hall.

"Hi, my name is Dr. Neil Gallagher. There's a debate that's going to happen in this room right after class at about 10:10. The thesis of the debate is, 'Suffering and pain are not compatible with the loving God described in the Bible; therefore, there is no God, and the Bible is false.' That thesis is affirmed by Dr. William Morrison of the Philosophy Department[48] and opposed by me. I am a philosopher, Brown University, and I have been invited by the Boulder church and the Christian Club to speak on these issues. Everyone is welcome to stay. It'll be right here in your illustrious chemistry auditorium."

They stayed.

A few bolted during the break, to haul in friends.

---

48 Sound familiar? "University of Colorado," "Philosophy Department." It's where Professor Victor J. Stenger holds court and indoctrinates students. Stenger is the author of *God: The Failed Hypothesis.*

Standing room only.

Tom Brook, president of the Christian College Club and coordinator of this event, sat to the right of the chemistry lab table, next to me. Professor Morrison to the left of the table.

10:10.

Tom walks to the lectern for introductions and rules.

I'd had these discussions before. Fought it out in many classrooms. I knew the five attacks of atheism… Which was Morrison going to use?

1) Christians do good things so they can earn their way to Heaven. Christians are as self-serving as anyone else. Don't give me this stuff about compassion. Christians have to be good boys and girls, so they don't go to Hell. There's no God of love up there in Heaven (wherever that is) inspiring them to do good works just for the sake of doing something good. It's all fear-driven… fire insurance.

2) The history of Christianity is the history of violence and bloodshed. Hitler was a Christian. Look at the Inquisition and slavery… all Christian activities. There is no God of justice or love in the Christian experience. There no God of justice or love, period.

3) You can't believe anything that's invisible. Christians believe in something that's invisible and non-provable. This is so evident that it's an insult to anyone with intelligence to have to point it out.

4) The Bible is archaic, stupid, sexist, rambling, violent, counterproductive, and irrelevant. And arrogant. One God? ONE God?! Naïve, narrow, and prejudicial. All roads lead to Heaven—if there is one. All the so-called sacred books are equally good.

5) The big one: There could never be a so-called God of love who allows suffering and pain.

My experience had been that, in these discussions, atheists rarely engage the eight classical proofs for the existence of God:

- Ontological

- Cosmological
- Aesthetic
- Moral
- Experiential
- Historical
- Archeological
- Scientific

These eight classical truths, I guessed, would probably be ignored by Morrison. My guess was that he'd grab the five attacks, which I knew from earlier debates were old, tired, false, anecdotal, inflammatory, and popular with atheists.

But let's see what he's going to say…

Morrison runs to the lectern. He firmly grips the slanted wooden slate, tightens his jaw, locks his eyes, and moves his head in a wide semicircle, demanding all students focus on him. "Thank you for coming. I assume you are here because you want the truth. I will say some things that will offend some people in this room. I will say some things that hurt. Again, I assume you're here because you want to hear the truth. If you cannot stand to hear the truth, I suggest that you leave. I welcome this opportunity because it's way past time to point out that all the abuses in recorded history came about because of God and religion. Whatever you call It, Them, or Her. In Western Civilization, people use God to thwart scientific research and scientific progress. Priests, preachers, popes, and kings use God to promote their selfish and dictatorial ends, and they still do in many places unless they are exposed and stopped. What I'm going to put out today—and I can only deal with some of the arguments—all I can do is say that belief in God is a dangerous and deceptive delusion. People who use God for their authority cannot be trusted. They must be silenced, and they must be stopped. If that means embarrassing you or embarrassing Dr. Gallagher, so be it.

"These Christians are always saying that pain and suffering do not disabuse the existence of a loving God. They say that because they can always say that pain or suffering is in some way purifying or redeemable. They're always saying that something good comes out of it even though it really hurts.

"Really hurts: cancer, tornadoes, heart attacks, the Holocaust, poverty—doesn't matter. The more painful it is, the nicer God is, or something like that. It's all purifying down the road, by and by, or in the sweet by and by, as they like to sing in their songs.

"We will shatter that notion forever.

"WE WILL SHATTER THAT NOTION FOREVER!

"A forest fire, and deep in the forest is a fawn trapped in a cave. He burns to death. Pain. Random, unredemptive pain and suffering. That's pain pure and simple. There's no purifying future. There's no redemption down the road. This innocent fawn through no fault of its own burns to death. Where is God? Answer: Nowhere, because there is none. You can't divorce the two in the Christian way of looking at things. The Christian perspective is that they go together. There is a God, and He, She, or It is a God of love. So when you disavow the one, you disavow the other. There is no God of love because there is no God, and this unmitigated and excruciating suffering on the part of a fawn burning in a forest is one of millions of examples to show that. Millions of examples of pain and suffering that are going on all around the world right now. Where is God in all this?"

Morrison launched from there into a tirade on the Holocaust, the drought in Sudan, child molesting, AIDS, leukemia, and dozens of other brutalities and tragedies flashed on the headlines of daily papers. At the end of his 20-minute explosion, he returned to his theme: Unredemptive suffering is *ipso facto* proof that there is no God of love and no God. You can hope, you can wish, but hoping and wishing is not the same as facts. Christians do not think. Christians do not want to think about these things. Christians do not care. They do not care about people. They care about controlling people.

"I'm sorry. I told you it would be rough and said you could leave if you wanted to. After this is over, I invite you to join me and a few others who are brave enough to speak out and point out that this God stuff is a fraud."

I was stunned.

Stunned by his vitriolic delivery dripping with venom and hatred. I was stunned by this novel approach to pain and suffering, invoking the sentimental image of a barbecued Bambi. What was I going to say?

I felt like Bill Hybels sitting in back of that song leader as they both faced thousands of Hindus and Moslems on an open field in Bombay. "My praying," said Bill, "took on new earnestness. *O Lord, deliver me. Make it rain. Make me disappear. Make something happen here!* The mountain looked so tall and IMPOSSIBLE that I saw no point in asking God to move it. I would be content if it would simply cave in on me and put me out of my misery.

"I was a faint-hearted, doubt-filled, faith-starved pastor, but I spoke with Spirit-given confidence that night—confidence based solely on God's sufficiency to overcome the impossible. I spoke, and as I was speaking, I knew God was working. I ended the message and an invitation was given for people to trust Christ."[49]

But now it was my turn.

I sat there facing 510 shell-shocked students, eyes and ears frozen, waiting for me to say something factual and (maybe) hopeful. No, they never said that, but there was a palpable sense of anticipation. I faced 15 gloating faculty who seemed to be saying, "Gotcha." I felt their thoughts: "OK, so what is this Ivy air-head going to say now?"

Still in my chair, I dropped my head and prayed Asa adapted for this crisis:

<blockquote>
Help us—Help me, O God, for there is none like You
to help the weak conquer the strong.
We're here—I'm here to meet this huge army
because I trust in You and who You are.
</blockquote>

---

49 Bil Hybels, Lavonne Neff, and Ashley Wiersman, *Too Busy Not To Pray: Slowing Down to Be With God* (Downers Grove, IL: IVP Books, 2008) page 8

Don't let mere mortals intimidate and brainwash those in this room
Who may have open hearts and open minds and who really want answers.

I stood and walked to the podium. My stomach hurt, like someone had just rammed the blunt end of a telephone pole into my navel. I raised my hands to the side of the wooden slate. I slid salty palms up and down the sides of the corner ledges. It felt like it was a full minute before I could raise my hands to the top of the wooden slate. I had no idea what I was going to say.

I heard these words come from my mouth:

"Thank you, Professor Morrison, and that was a category mistake.

"What's a category mistake? Oh, and thank all of you for your integrity and patience in sitting here in the pursuit of truth. What's a category mistake? Before I go into that, I do want to thank Professor Morrison for his novel argument and for identifying himself as an atheist.

"That is honest.

"Many people hide under euphemistic labels: skeptic, agnostic, doubter. That really means they are closet atheists. Either you're a theist— in my definition that means you recognize the existence of God and your accountability to Him, i.e. the God of the Bible, or you're an atheist and you refuse to recognize His existence and your accountability.

"I really do respect Professor Morrison for his forthright admission: "I am an atheist," he said. "There is no compromise; there is no middle ground. You've heard the story of the dying atheist who called his son to his bedside, and, to make sure that no one attempted to convert him, told his son to grab a Magic Marker and write above his bed, 'God is nowhere.'" In his haste, the son spaced out the words.

The visiting chaplain said, "Sir, I see that you've had a change in heart. I see above your bed, 'God is now here.'"

"There is no middle ground. There is no fuzziness. Either you embrace the truth, 'God is nowhere,' or you embrace the truth, 'God is now here.'

"Whichever… there are consequences.

"And consequences are dramatized in behavior."

- Behavior betrays belief, and

- Action dramatizes conviction.

"Every action at its root dramatizes whether a person believes in God or does not. It was Mortimer Adler, editor-in-chief of the Encyclopedia Britannica, who said, 'More consequences for thought and action follow the affirmation or denial of God than from answering any other basic question.'

"There's no middle ground. Either you believe in a transcendent, intimate, and loving God who wants to live His life of love and power and purpose through you, and a God, by the way, to whom you're accountable. Or you don't believe in that God. Professor Morrison has said that he does not believe in God and boldly calls himself an atheist and his position atheism. Thank you for that clarity.

"Let's make something else clear: We're not here for academic tennis, back and forth, back and forth, back and forth. At least, in my view, we're not. The deeper moral issue—Well, let me make a statement and ask a question. Anyone in this room who has never sinned, please stand up."

I returned to my seat. I looked up. Nobody stood except one. Happened to be smack in the middle of the room: a tall, bearded white guy with an Afro haircut. Looked like a globe of white foam atop two columns, shoulders thrown back hard and stiff, cradling two massive arms up against his chest. He glared at me. (The reason Mr. Afro never sinned, I later learned, is because he never did anything that he did not want to do. That was Mr. Afro's definition of sin, the definition of sin for millions of deceived people in America: If you submit to authority, especially religious authority, THAT's a sin.)

I continued. "We're here not only to discuss the transcendental reality of an infinite God, but to point out that the infinite God we're talking about came to us in the person of Jesus Christ to take on the sin of everyone in this room. I'll talk more about this in the lecture series coming up this week in the next four nights at the Boulder church.

"The category mistake," I continued, "is a fancy word for what we call the difference between apples and oranges. You know, someone says the stock market is going up today because it's going to rain."

You say, "That's apples and oranges." No comparison. No relevance.

"Philosophers have a way of describing things that defy common sense. In describing a certain tool, philosophers say: 'This is a perfectly balanced shaft, attached to a triangular instrument at the bottom, forged in such a way that its angle protrudes from a fulcrum, which enables the owner to have the least muscular resistance and enjoy the least amount of effort in moving one part of earth to another part of earth.'

"Common sense says: 'That's a shovel.' A category mistake is a fancy way of saying that your comparison doesn't work because it's apples and oranges.

"Professor Morrison—and by the way, this discussion is no reflection of Professor Morrison. I honor him as a scholar. It is his position that is weak and indefensible. His position is a round peg in a square hole or a square peg in a round hole. His conundrum of a barbecued Bambi bears no relation to reality.

"Here's another category mistake… a clever game that has sucker-punched many of us: If a tree falls in the forest and no one's around, does it make a noise? Answer: 'Well, no, because there's no one there to hear it,' or 'Well, I don't really know, because there's no one there to hear it.'

"This is a category mistake. There are two laws operating here. Two separate laws. (1) When a tree falls in a forest and hits the ground, it emits sound waves. Those sound waves are emitted independent of a receiver. Laws of physics explode into action when one object hits another. (2) And laws of physics are operational when sound waves hit an eardrum.

"These are two different categories: (1) sound waves emitted by colliding forces, for instance the tree hitting the forest floor, and (2) sound waves processed by an eardrum.

"The person who says the tree does not make a noise has the burden of proof on him! What would have caused the suspension of the laws of physics, so that sound waves were not emitted from the crashing tree? Or what would have interfered with the laws of physiology and audiology that would have prevented the hammer and stirrup, in the middle ear, from processing sound waves? The burden of proof is on the ostensibly clever person who tosses this puzzle at us.

"We reject it because it is a category mistake.'

"The underlying assumption of the crashing-tree puzzle is that there is no reality unless there is perception. But that's false, because truth exists independent of:

perception ,

appreciation,

or acknowledgement.

"For my philosophy friends in the audience," I continued, "You know that Kant made this mistake on a grand scale in *The Critique of Pure Reason* when he differentiated between noumena and phenomena. Truth out there and truth down here. Phenomena is merely our perception of truth, and thus... gradually... came the belief that everything is relative. The extension of this fallacy to our discussion today is that there is no absolute truth... especially no absolute truth about the existence of a loving God.

"Let's return to Morrison and the story of the barbecued Bambi. It's a category mistake. We don't know if there is now or ever was a fawn trapped in a burning cave. Morrison's example is purely hypothetical... a fancy word for saying it's a fable, a myth... has no relation to reality.

"BUT YOU'RE NOT HERE BECAUSE OF A FOREST FABLE! You are here because you have questions about 'Why was I born? What am I doing here? Where am I going?' You are here because you have thoughts ricocheting in your brain.

- I just found out I'm pregnant. What am I going to do?
- How am I going to get home? I don't have enough money for gas.
- Which parent am I going to live with now that they're getting a divorce?
- How do I get through this pain of being dumped? The guy said he loved me.
- What if I get a B rather than an A in Political Science? I'll never get into law school.
- What is *my* purpose in life?

"And on and on and on. Those are your questions. Is there a God out there who cares? Is there a God out there who has solutions?

"Yes, there is a God of love. It is not a fable. It is an existential and immediate and practical issue. The Bible dramatizes a God of love whose principles, when practiced, PREVENT problems and whose principles, when practiced, turn problems into something positive, therapeutic, and triumphant.

"One part of Morrison's exposition is true. The God of the Bible does turn pain into purpose. Victor Frankl, the Jewish psychiatrist who was tortured in a Nazi concentration camp, said, 'All suffering can be endured if it is imbued with meaning.'

"Thoughtful people—compassionate people—don't invest time ranting about a barbecued Bambi that does not exist. That does not help anyone. Rather, we accept that suffering is a fact and look for ways to help people with that painful fact.

"As I mentioned in the case with the crashing tree, the same is true in this case: the burden of proof is on the disputant to show that there was or is a barbecued Bambi and to show what relevance that fable has to do with MY birth, purpose, destiny."

I sat down.

Birth...

Purpose...

destiny.

Sounds poetic... 't's got rhythm. Where'd that come from? Thank you, God.

Morrison returned to the lectern. "I'm not going to split hairs into whether there was a burning Bambi or not, a rather insensitive and cavalier reference on Dr. Gallagher's part, I might add. I don't think it takes much imagination for any of us to know it's very likely that in forest fires, there is unredeemed suffering all the time. The more obvious case against the alleged good and loving God is the third part of the predicate, God. We won't go into the suffering and pain and violence that have been caused by people who believe in this God. It was Dr. Gallagher who dismissed that as being ad hominem and as being inconsistent with the perfect life of Jesus, a favorite tactic of so-called apologists. But even though it veers from our agreed upon premise, the obvious has to be stated. The third part of his predicate refers to God. He or She or It is absolutely, totally invisible.

Invisible then and invisible now. To believe in a loving God is like believing in a loving Santa Claus. Santa Claus is a jolly old elf who loves everybody, gives everybody gifts. But there is no Santa Claus. It's only a childish myth, and everyone knows that. God is invisible. It's a given.

"Dr. Gallagher talked about common sense. It's an obscenity to believe, really believe, in the fairy godmother, angels, Santa Claus, the Easter bunny, Peter Pan, or God. You can't see Him, or It, or She, or touch or smell or feel. This is so obvious. It violates everything we know about science and reason, and because He or She or It is invisible, He or She or It has been used for centuries to control people, to tell them that Mr. Invisible said that women, or children, or blacks have no rights. I'm sorry, but I told you at the beginning that this would be rough and I'd get right to it. If you believe in God, you're following along with what your mother told you, and it's out of respect for her or some family tradition or some social necessity, but you're still doing it. Thank you." He sat down.

He leaped to the lectern again: "And since we're getting all the truth out here, preachers and people like them use Mr. Invisible to collect a lot of money. They collect a lot of money and build empires for themselves."

For ten minutes, Morrison lectured us on the scandals of televangelists and pedophile priests.

My turn. "Thank you again, Professor Morrison, for not backing away on your stand on atheism. In an earlier essay, I address these issues in an article entitled, 'People Who Think for Themselves Are the People Who Become Christians.' In our agreement, that was not the topic we were to discuss tonight. I'm tempted to ignore your passionate sermon, because as you admitted, you have violated our agreed-upon premise that we'd stick to the issue of how the alleged pain and suffering of the mythical fawn disabused the notion of God. You've gone far afield from that, and I have no obligation to go out into that field, nor do I want to waste the time of the thoughtful men and women who are here.

But you've forced me.

You've made it necessary for me to expose the fallacies in your sermon against God. I have to take the opportunity to expose the fallacies in your tirade against God. I have to take the opportunity to expose your fallacies

, else people will leave the room thinking that (a) there is no answer, or (b) those fallacies are unassailable.

"Your major underlying premise is all things not accessible by the five senses (visible, audible, tactile, etc.) are things that are not real. God is not accessible to the five senses; ergo, God is not real.

"In that major premise of yours, electricity is not real. No one can see, touch, smell, taste electricity. We do see, smell, touch the effects of electricity. The other flaw in your premise is its obverse: all items that are accessible to sight, smell, touch, taste are real. But the flaw in that argument is the following: take a large beaker of clear water, put into it a ruler, and anyone sitting on the outside looking at it is convinced that the ruler is crooked. The eyes see a crooked ruler, because our senses are fallible. Mirages, optical illusions, double vision, refractive lighting. Daily experience reminds us that the five senses are fallible and are not an exclusive and reliable way to know anything, and that destroys Professor Morrison's premise.

"Knowing means: <u>justified true belief</u>. It is belief on which you base actions. And Christian actions have been shown to be helpful in achieving positive, worthwhile goals, and by Christian actions, I mean those consistent with the life and teaching of Jesus Christ.

"One could argue, but it's not the point of this discussion—I will be discussing some of these issues in my lecture series at the Boulder church over the next four nights— that there are ways that we <u>do know</u> God that transcend the five senses. There are ways that we know many things that transcend the five senses and are unverifiable by the five senses. Why, we can't even quantify, according to the five senses, the phenomena called love. No one in this room denies the reality of love. It's real, and it's intangible. It's a force and a feeling that is rock-certain, just like a rock that you can wrap your five fingers around.

"Since Professor Morrison brought up the topic, what's real—A real force called love comes from a real person whom we call God, who demonstrated His Love to us in Jesus Christ, and offers forgiveness and a renewed life to all of us in this room. Will you accept it?" (There was a small smattering of applause on that one. Hallelujah. There were some Christians in the audience.)

I sat and I prayed. *"Thank you, God, for loving to do the impossible for people who make themselves available."*

* * * * * * * * *

Epilogue: After the discussion, I approached Professor Morrison and extended my hand to shake his: "I'd love to get together with you for breakfast or coffee in the morning, so we can just talk shop or anything else you'd like to talk about. I would love to hear about your dissertation. I know that was a lot of work. I enjoyed having this discussion."

"No, thanks. I don't eat with people like you."

So much for the magnanimous attitude of atheists (well, some atheists) who claim you don't need God to be good.

The next four nights were packed at the Boulder church auditorium where I discussed, "People Who Think for Themselves Are the People Who Become Christians."

…and praying Asa the whole time.

* * * * * * * * *

1I - Asa Stops Suicide

1I - Asa Stops Suicide

She looked 80, but from the information she would later give me, she was only 53.

She stopped crying when I told her my mother committed suicide.

Didn't know I was going to say it.

Shocked me when I heard it.

Asa made me do it.

Like yellow, stinking bile swirling in a nauseous belly, her story made my stomach churn with my own memories of pain, grief, and confusion.

Mrs. Sousa's story: Religious leaders, as well as family and friends, of her Portuguese traditions had scolded her and ostracized her, telling her that suicide was shame, suicide was Hell, suicide was Judas.

Her son had committed suicide.

No Mass for him. A secret graveside service. She knew where the cemetery plot was but had never visited. Eight years, and she still wore black on her body, blacker by the day with depression. A gray film covered her face, grayer by the day with age and shame.

"Take a deep breath, Mrs. Sousa, and start wherever you want."

"I've got to talk to you about something. They say you help people." (I was pastoring a church outside Boston while finishing my doctoral studies.)

L-o-n-g pause. I looked at her and asked, "May I hold your hand."

She nodded. I lay my right hand on top of her quivering left hand resting on my desk, and she exploded. "WHY? Why did he do that to us? We loved him. He was young. He had his whole life to live. He had a good life. He was so young. He's in Hell now. No one comes around anymore. They don't ask Tony to help at the Knights anymore. We don't take communion anymore. He was so young. He had everything to live for. What did we do wrong? Why did he do that? Why did he do that to himself? Why did he do that to us? Why? Why? Why? It's no accident, is it, when you put a gun inside your mouth and pull the trigger? He killed himself. Why?"

"*He*, I guess means your... son?"

"Ramon. Eighteen years old. Why does an 18-year-old kill himself?"

"Do you want to tell me how it happened?" I paused.

And I prayed Asa out loud with Mrs. Sousa and for Mrs. Sousa:

> Help us, O God, for there is none like You
> to help the weak conquer the strong.
> We're here to meet this huge army of pain and despair.
> I don't know what to say or do to help, but
> I trust in You and who You are.
> Don't let Satan's attacks torment this woman any longer.

"Mrs. Sousa, my mother committed suicide. I have been there. Mrs. Sousa, people who commit suicide don't know what they're doing. Something snaps. It was not your fault.

It was not your fault.

It was not your fault.

Something snaps inside of them that kills that divine passion for self-preservation. I don't know why, in some circles, suicide is a family stigma. I don't know why your church did what it did. I don't know why some people shun families who have suffered the trauma of suicide."

Until then, I had never had the occasion to tell anyone that Mother, Rita T. Gallagher, had committed suicide. Didn't know if I would ever tell anyone. Suicide has stigma. Stays with you, like a port wine stain smearing your forehead and cheeks.

Always there.

But why does it have more stigma, or invite more condemnation, than adultery, theft, greed, gluttony, or lying? All sins.

"Mrs. Sousa, we don't know what was in your son's mind? His name again...?"

"Ramon… Tony's my husband."

"We don't know what was in Ramon's mind when he shoved the gun up to the roof of his mouth and let it go. You and I don't know if he had OD'ed on something. We don't know. We leave that in the hands of a merciful God. What we do know is that you're not responsible for it. God gives people free will. We do know that there are people who need you now, that God needs you now. We're going to talk about healing for you, and help for you, and the help that you'll be able to give other people. We're going to take care of this now. Let's go."

I took her by the elbow and escorted her from my office. We walked down the front steps of the church building into a wet and chilly March wind. "Get into my car. We're going to the cem—"

"No, No—"

"Yes, Mrs. Sousa. If you want to talk to me again, we're going there now."

We drove through the old part of the city and passed Our Lady of Heaven Cemetery. They wouldn't let him be buried there. We drove until we got to City Cemetery. I stopped at the guard gate and asked for directions to the plot for Ramon Sousa.

Row L, Plot 11. We drove through hills of graves and wreaths and vaults and found Row 11. We parked on the side of a narrow cemetery path, the wheels sinking into the soft, muddy ground.

I put my arm around her as we walked past rows of tombstones, reading the headings, Alsace Bureé, Frederick Buffington, Antonio Balboa, Mary Duffey, Gloria Portea, Stanley Mills, and then…

Ramon Sousa,

A slab in the ground, the name barely visible.

She collapsed on the grass in a kneeling position, then bent forward and placed her head reverently against the tombstone. And exploded: "I hate you. I hate you. I hate you. How could you have done this to US? Ramon, my baby, we love you, we love you, we love you. We miss you so much. We were here for you. Why did you do this?"

She rained tears on the grave, nose in the wet grass, head pressing against the small concrete marker.

I knelt beside her, stroking the back of her neck and her shoulders. "It's going to be okay, Mrs. Sousa, it's going to be okay."

When her wailing and crying was spent, I lifted her and led her back to the car.

My turn to talk.

"Mrs. Sousa, may I say something?" I asked while handing her a stack of yellow Wendy's napkins piled on my dashboard. "Mrs. Sousa, this visit was good. I'm proud of you. It was good for you; it was good for me. I remember getting that call that my mother had descended the stairs into a dark cellar, placed a rope around her neck, and leaped off the stairs, snapping her neck and killing her instantly. Why?

"I don't know why. I knew that I had done everything I could for her, and I had no idea she was contemplating suicide. Mrs. Sousa, this visit has been like taking a needle and puncturing a boil for you and for me, for both of us. Stinky yellow puss came out, and infection drained from my body. I—"

"I'm glad we came, too. Thank you, Dr.… Mr.… Reverend….???"

"Just Neil is fine."

We drove back to the church.

Didn't hear from Mrs. Sousa for three years. One Friday night in a crowded Stop 'n' Shop, she was checking out.

There were two people in front of me in the line. She was number three.

Barely recognized her. She looked 53 now, not 83. Earrings, bronze-tan complexion, elegantly coiffed hair, sculptured blouse, pressed tan slacks.

"Mrs. Sousa?"

She looked at me, smiled. "It's Mr. Gallagher—Mr. Neil? Yes?" she said with a smile. She turned to the young woman clutching a baby beside her. "Marguerite, this is that Mr. Neil, the one who took me to the cemetery that day. I talked to him about Ramon a long time ago. This is my new grandson, Geraldo." She took her bag of groceries and switched packages with her daughter. Her daughter handed over Geraldo, and Mrs. Sousa hoisted him directly in front of me to make SURE I saw her bouncing prize. She turned to the clerk, "Okay, you can help us out with our groceries." She followed the clerk out the door as she said over her shoulder, "We're on our way to the beach for the weekend."

Nothing else…

And that's okay. Guess she's moving forward.

Wish I had known Asa 50 years ago.

Wish Mother had known Asa 70 years ago.

Rita Teresa Donahue Gallagher. At 17, she left her native Lawrence, Mass, headed for the Big Apple. Her mother, Grammy, said, "I'm never going to tell you what to do, so if you get in trouble, you can't blame me. Do what you want." Little did Grammy know about the power of loving discipline and daily accountability within a family.

"A man reaps what he sows." (Galatians 6:7)

At 17, Rita bussed to New York, this petite, pretty brunette full of life, and grabbed a job as a telephone operator. Jobs were plentiful. The workforce was dedicated to WWII efforts.

She dated a New York firefighter. Nice home on Long Island. They married and gave birth to Robert Philip Doorley, followed two years later by William Neil Doorley.

Robbie and Neily.

Four years into the marriage, the firefighter found someone he thought was prettier. He dumped us. I was three at the time.

No job, no support, no education. She hoists Robbie and Neily in her arms and busses us from New York to Boston, and Boston to Lawrence.

A divorced woman.

In the 1940s Catholic church, divorce and remarriage was a big no-no, and it didn't matter if you were the cause of divorce or the victim of divorce (as Rita T. was).

Bumped into an old classmate, Francis Gallagher. At 35, he was diabetic and a drunk, I'm told, but he loved her, and she wanted the companionship. They married. He adopted Robbie and Neily, now Robbie and Neily Gallagher. They gave birth to Frankie Gallagher. This stepfather, Francis Gallagher, worked in a slave shop in a filthy, old, dangerous textile mill on Broadway Avenue in Lawrence, memorialized in Alan Farnham's book:

There are no "Café Budapests" in Lawrence... the section where mills were located was considered by locals to be among the city's toughest, a wasteland of shuttered sops and broken windows...

Life for working men and women in Lawrence had never been easy. The city was the scene for 1912's Bread and Roses strike by 25,000 workers, but at least the city had once bustled with commercial activity. Now, it ranked 24th among the poorest cities in the United States, no longer famous for manufacturing, but for being a crack-cocaine capital and a magnet for newly arrived immigrants. Though only 30 miles north of Boston, it might as well have been in the third world.[50]

Irish revelry demanded whiskey parties on Friday night. After each, her drunken brothers stumbled over to our tenement and beat her up. Something to do. Drunken Francis was out cold. They locked Robbie and me in our room.

Rita's pain, like a feverish thermometer, is rising.

TB and diabetes drained Francis's health. They shipped him off to the sanatorium. We plunged into welfare, living on powdered milk, moldy bread, and brick-hard surplus cheese. Rita Teresa Donahue Gallagher scraped together pennies to buy sequins and trinkets and glued together handmade earrings. We went door-to-door selling them.

Five years later, Francis is released. The priest tells him he can't live with Rita. She's a divorced woman, see? He goes into forced isolation.

Rita's pain is rising. Eventually, Francis's love for Rita overrides any doctrinal jail. Francis J. and Rita escape the guilt and shame of divorce. They are reunited and happy. Six months, and he swoons again into a diabetic coma.

He was not going to drink anymore, he said. "I'll take care of myself, and I'll take my medicine." But that morning, they overslept. She woke

---

50Farnham, Alan, *Forbes: Great Success Stories* Forbes,, Inc. (New York: John Wiley and Sons, 2000) 4.

and found him swooning off in a coma. Orange juice. Sugared water. He coughed, gurgled and swallowed. Looked routine. We waited. No response. More orange juice, more sugared water. Wouldn't go down. It filled and overflowed his open mouth, like racing tap water overflowing a full glass. Streams of orange spilled over his blue-gray lips, cascading down his salt-and-pepper stubbled chin. Too late. The doctor later said his heart simply could stand no more comas.

I was 15 then, and watched him die in Mother's lap. She was sitting; he was propped up. Frantically, she rubbed her hands up and down his back, back and forth across his caved-in chest, trying to revive him. His mustard-yellow face fell back; his cold, damp body hung across her arms. Propping him up again, she rained tears on his motionless body, like David's *Pietá*—Mary in agony over a limp, cold form.

Funeral and burial arrangements were dictated by others. (Poverty's lousy for handling death.) We had no choice. No money. No insurance.

Rita's pain is rising.

She got a job: $40 a week. We couldn't afford our wood-rotted tenement. I looked for full-time work, but Mother insisted I stay in school. I finished high school. She insisted I attend college. I found 40 hours of work at night and earned a degree during the day. Tuition, $100 a year. Somehow we scraped it together.

After graduation, I joined the Peace Corps and lived on survival wages. Nursing and teaching in those leper colonies in Northern Thailand, I lived on $50 a month (made $75 and sent $25 home).

I return home and find Rita T. drowning in depression. Someone who hated alcohol, she grabs vodka and guzzles it. She locks herself in her room, coming out only for snacks and trips to the store to buy more booze. She won't speak to us. She won't speak to anybody.

Rita's pain is rising.

Frankie goes off to the service, Bob to Washington for an embassy job. I tell her I'll stay. She says, "No."

I grab her attention as she darts from bedroom to refrigerator. "I'm staying, Mother. I'm staying here with you. I had no idea."

She says, "No, go off and do your own life." She won't be dissuaded. She screams and insists.

I hitchhike to Texas and enter graduate school.

Find a wonderful wife, establish a home, and bring Rita T. to Texas. Miracle of miracles. She agrees to come. We're going to drain the pain, start all over again.

She comes and stays three weeks. Fusses and fidgets and moans. Wants to return to her native Lawrence. Says she can make it on her own. She'll live with friends, she says. I arrange for friends to meet her at the airport and reluctantly put her on a plane.

Six months later comes the call. I'm in the library writing a paper. I am paged. I pick up the phone. "Please call Sergeant Michael Broward at the Lawrence Police Department."

I called.

"We found your mother hanging in a cellar, an apparent suicide," the detective tells me, right to the point. "I am so sorry. We've contacted your brothers."

I return to Lawrence for the cleanup and the funeral. Judging from the vodka bottles at the bottom of the cellar stairs, secured windows and locks, the position of the rope, and the note, "No burden, no more, no pain to anyone," I draw my own conclusion that it's a suicide.

Mercifully and deliberately, Detective Broward "loses" the suicide note. Cause of death: accident. Additional details: none. He wants the family to have the dignity of a Christian burial and no embarrassing notices in the paper.

These events drive me to study suicide. I learn that it touches millions. I learn three truths:

1. Asa stops suicide. Had Rita Teresa Donahue Gallagher claimed:

> Help me, O God, for there is none like You
> to help the weak conquer the strong.
> I'm here facing this huge army of fear, worry, and sadness.
> I trust in You and who You are.
> Don't let my failures, rejections, and depression
> stand against You and Your loving purposes for me.

...she would have enjoyed, early on, the promise: GOD LOVES TO DO THE IMPOSSIBLE. No heartache, depression, abandonment, fear, or pain is beyond the reach of a God who conquers million-man armies. God is a God of solutions. The bigger the problem, the bigger the solution. He turns pain into purpose.

2. Don't condemn families struck by suicide. Don't even think of them as being "tainted" by suicide. Don't be judgmental or harsh or condemnatory. No one knows what went through that person's head. What we do know is this: people who commit suicide have snapped. God's passion for self-preservation is so strong and so compelling, a sane person does not commit suicide. Something snaps.

3. Don't do it.

   Don't do it.

   Don't do it.

   Claim Asa. With every challenge, with every attack of fear, pain, shame, or depression, claim Asa: (a) It's the right thing to do, and (b) It's a powerful, proven strategy, and (c) claiming Asa will prevent you from committing the most selfish act of your life. Think that suicide prevents problems?

   Uh uh.

   Creates problems. It leaves others tormented with guilt and grief. So right now while you're in your sane mind, claim this: "What I've got and where I am is plenty good enough to build again, and with God's help, there is always a solution."

The *Wall Street Journal*[51] in its article, "One Taliban Bullet, Two Lives Lost," tells the tragic story of U.S. Army Medic, Spc. Keith Benson.

> Between 2004—one year after the U.S.-led invasion of Iraq—and 2010, the rate of self-inflicted deaths among active-duty Army personnel rose from 9.6 per 100,000 to 21.8 per 100,000, surpassing the civilian rate in the U.S. for the first time in 2008, according to a U.S. Army study released this year...
>
> At Spc. Benson's memorial service, his fellow soldiers had no answers. They wondered why he hadn't asked them for help. Some were angry at him for adding an intentional death to so many unavoidable ones...
>
> The mood was different this time: grief, anger and confusion, said the soldiers who attended...
>
> Sgt. Wolfington, the senior medic, was angry. "He had a lot more options," he said. "There's always people to talk to"...

As the tragic story of Keith Benson dramatized:

Don't do suicide.

Suicide claims more victims—many more victims that the guy (or gal) who pulls the trigger or swallows the bottle.

Claim the power of Asa to grab solutions, enrich your life, and rescue you from despair.

You and others.

---

51 Michael M. Philips, "One Taliban Bullet, Two Lives Lost," *Wall Street Journal,*, Saturday/ Sunday edition, May 26-27, 2012, pp.A5, A10.

A man—or woman—ignited by courage and committed to Asa action is unstoppable. And he or she empowers others to be equally compassionate, courageous and unstoppable, no matter the obstacle. That's the claim.

That's the power.

That's the promise of Asa.

The Asa Prayer
Help us, O God, for there is none like You
to help the weak conquer the strong.
We're here to meet this huge army
because we trust in You and who You are.
Don't let mere mortals stand against You.

* * * * * * * * *

I hear a little murmuring:

"Too good to be true."

"Makes God a genie. Pray Asa and God pops out."

"Life's not like that. You're insulting my intelligence and toying with my faith."

…mmmm…

God's God. Can do whatever He wants. Can respond when and how He wants. He's not a genie.

I know all that.

I also know there's truth in this anecdote you've heard from a speaker or preacher somewhere:

> Brother Smith pays attention one Sunday morning when the pastor's expounding on prayer. He reminds his congregation: "I can do all things through Christ." "With God, all things are possible." "You have not because you ask not."
>
> So… Brother Smith, beginning Sunday evening, passionately prays. He kneels at his kitchen chair, slaps elbows and forearms on the seat, bends forward, knits his fingers together, and rests his head on the chair frame:
>
> "God, I need a million dollars. I'm asking you; let me win the lottery. I'll give You the credit. And I'll tithe it. Let me win the lottery."
>
> Comes the lottery notices on Friday. No win.
>
> Sunday evening again and prayer time:
>
> "God, I need a million dollars. I'm asking you; let me win the lottery. I'll give You the credit. And I'll tithe it. Let me win the lottery."
>
> Comes Friday. No win.
>
> Sunday evening again.
>
> "God, this is the third time. I'm begging, pleading, asking… like You say to do. Let me win the lottery. I *need* the million dollars!"
>
> Friday night comes and goes. No win.

Once more, in desperation:

"God, I know you're my loving Father. Ple-e-eze let me win the lottery. Don't abandon me in my time of need."

And a voice booms from the ceiling:

"I hear you, my son. Gimme a break. Buy a ticket!"

Buy a ticket: Say, "God make my life a miracle of Your service."

And when the million- man armies slam you (as they surely will), buy a ticket: pray Asa and ACT on it.

- Whether you're
- Agent or editor
- Buyer or browser
- Parent or child
- Teacher or student
- Book collector or gift-giver

Say it and enjoy it:

"God, make my life a miracle of Your service."

The impossible armies will come. And you'll get to claim Asa and see the power of God flow through you in love and service and victory.

Head → Heart → Hand.

The Prayer of Asa:

Believe it in your HEAD.

Ignite it in your HEART.

Release it in your HANDS of service.

With no apologies to Don Quixote…

The Impossible Prayer

To Pray the Impossible Prayer
To press on when you're feeling so low,
To believe with unquenchable trust,
To proceed when fatigue screams, "No! No!"

To love people too much to quit,
To claim Asa when everything's grim,
To admit you can't do it alone,
To surrender ALL power and purpose to Him.

No matter how scared you feel now,
This is God's plea:
"Claim Asa's prayer, and you'll know
That God is still there for you and for me.

To smack the Impossible right in the eye,
To stun all the critics with this:
"I'll trust God or die."

You know when you use this incredible power,
Satan and his demons immediately cower.

Go! The Lord's looking for that woman or man,
Blasting the "self-help" poisonous air.
Who praise and who shout, "Tough folks seek God…"
And claim the Impossible Prayer.

Chapter 2

Asa: The Man

The Mission

The Message

Asa: The Man

Asa: a 14th-century English stained-glass window

Asa smacked Cush and crashed chariots.

Asa: The Man

Who was this guy who bellied up to one of the "baddest" warriors in the Bible in one of the bloodiest battles… and gave us one of the best prayers in the Bible?

Asa.

When Israelites heard the word Joshua, they knew it meant "savior." When they heard the word Jabez, they knew it meant "pain." When they heard the word Asa, they knew it meant "healer."

God used him to heal the land.

He was KING Asa. Ruling from 913 to 872 B.C., he succeeded his father King Abijah, King of Judah.

As the son of Abijah, he was the grandson of Rehoboam, the great-grandson of Solomon, and the great-great-grandson of David.

A great and godly heritage.

From his distant granddad David, Asa received his courage for battle. From his distant granddad Solomon, he received his divine wisdom to echo a divine prayer, the prayer of Asa.

Good granddad bloodline, going up.

He was also the distant granddad of Hezekiah, one of the godliest kings of Old Testament history. ("The Reforms of Hezekiah," 2 Chronicles 29, 30)

Good bloodline going down.

Asa was God's man and scored a perfect 10:

1.   "Asa was with the Lord." (2 Chronicles 15:2)
2.   This is fundamental.
3.   He accepted the charge from Azariah to be strong and do not give up. (2 Chronicles 15:7)
4.   He took courage. (2 Chronicles 15:8)

5. He acted. He removed the idols from Judah and Benjamin. (2 Chronicles 15:8)

6. He prepared the altar. (2 Chronicles 15:8)

7. He assembled all Judah, Benjamin, Ephraim, Manasseh, and Simeon and large numbers from Israel. They followed him in his obedience to the Lord. (2 Chronicles 15:9)

8. He entered into a covenant to seek the Lord God. (2 Chronicles 15:12)

9. "He threw Mama off the train," deposing his queen-mother Maacah for her idol worship. (2 Chronicles 15:16)

10. He followed his good lineage, the humble, praiseworthy attitude of David, expelling the male prostitutes and smashing idols. (2 Chronicles 14:2-7)

11. And finally, he defeated Zerah the Cushite claiming the power of his historic prayer. (2 Chronicles 14:11)

Asa: The Mission

Asa: The Mission

Zerah the Cushite marched out against them with a million men
and three hundred chariots, and came as far as Mareshah. 10 Asa
went out to meet him, and they took up battle positions in the
Valley of Zephathah near Mareshah.

—2 Chronicles 14:9-10 NIV

Poland's plan: crush Hitler's planes and panzers with people, ponies,
and pistols.

Right.

Go get 'em, Poland.

Didn't look like the resources of Asa would work, either. Text says that
he had 580,000 soldiers and his "pistols" were swords and daggers. Zerah
the Cushite had one-million fierce warriors and his "panzers" were chariots—300 of them, manned by savage drivers gripping iron shields and
standing shoulder to shoulder with their archery buddies ready to kill with
their one-million arrows.

Professor Jonathan P. Roth, in *War and World History*, nailed it: "In the
chariot revolution, warriors soon found out that swords and daggers were
no match for chariots carrying seasoned archers."[52]

That was because,

"Chariotry consisted of battle cars, which were heavy vehicles with
narrow bodies and tall fronts. The driver of the car sat ahead of the

52 Jonathon P. Roth, *War and World History: The Great Courses,* Disk 1, 2009.

warrior threw javelins attached to its sides. There were four solid disk wheels, each made of three sections joined together and held on to fixed axels by log cylinders, so the wheels could rotate independently of each other. These battle cars, drawn by four equids, could attain speeds of twelve miles and hour.[53]

Speed, superior weapons, and a super-power army is what Asa faced. Odds 2:1

Clearly, a Cushite slaughter. Swords vs. chariots.

Mission impossible.

It would be the biggest single massacre in one day, eclipsing the bombings of Hiroshima and Nagasaki , a future historic tragedy.

So, who were these Cushite charioteers and savage soldiers who turned the blood of enemies ice-cold with fear?

Referred to 54 times in the Bible, they were descendants—ironically—of Moses through Zipporah, the Midianite, also called the Cushite. Zipporah was the one, you remember, who hurled at Moses's feet a bloody foreskin of their son, following the ritual circumcision. Numbers 12 tells us that Miriam and Aaron grumbled against Moses for his association with Zipporah. (Maybe they knew something.)

Symbolically, the tension between the followers of Moses and the followers of Zipporah expanded and exploded over the centuries until the time of Asa.

A Cushite victory meant (1) death to Asa himself, (2) death to all the followers of Moses and Judah, and later Israel, (3) death to the divinely inspired monarchy, and (4) the probable death of monarchism itself.

A Cushite victory seemed certain:

Cushites were the backbone of the armies in the earliest ages. The Egyptian had no warlike qualities. It was the Cushite who was the head and brains of the foreign conquests. It was the Cushite element of the Old Empire that extended itself in foreign colonization eastward and westward around the world. Across Arabia

---

53 Simon Anglim,et al, *Fighting Techniques of the Ancient World 3000 BC – 500 AD* (New York: St. Martin's Press, 2002) 80-81.

and southwestern Asia, even to the central highlands, inscriptions and massive images in stone stand as voiceless witnesses that the Cushites were the commanders of the Egyptian armies. We must remember that in the early ages the Cushites were not a subject race but that their power as a great empire was at its zenith.[54]

Asa's mission was simple and scary:

(1) Crush this empire in one big battle;
(2) And thereby save the lineage and bloodline of Judah for the coming of the future Savior.

> The future of human redemption was in Asa's hands.
> And he didn't even know it.

54 Drusilla Dunjee Houston, *Wonderful Ethiopians of the Ancient Cushite Empire: Book I* (Bel Air: BiblioBazaar, 2007) 37-38.

Asa: The Message

"Follow me!" roared Asa, repeating his historic prayer.

And his men did.

Why? Why would they do that? Five-hundred-eighty thousand against an army of more than a million?

For every one of me, there are two of them.

I'm in the ring, and I see in the opposing corner TWO mad, muscular, and frothing hulks.

I say, "Time out, ref. This is not fair. I'll come back tomorrow when it's fair. First thing, they're a lot bigger than me. Secondly, there's two of them."

Not Asa, not his men. They didn't say that. They marched forward. "And the army of Judah triumphed as the Cushites fled."

How did they do that?

That's the message of the prayer of Asa: GOD LOVES TO DO THE IMPOSSIBLE, FOR MEN AND WOMEN WHO MAKE THEM-SELVES AVAILABLE.

And act on faith.

These are people we call leaders.

Asa dramatized leadership, and that's his message for all generations:

1. **Leaders act in spite of fear.**

    It's clear that Asa did not "feel" courageous when he appealed to God.

    The Hollywood depiction of courage is wrong: that Rambo-type who smashes any danger without fear or hesitation.

    Wrong.

Courage is acting in spite of fear.

2. **Leaders look to God rather than to circumstances.**

That's the whole point of the Asa prayer.

Charles Stanley loves to tell his story as a young pastor coached by an 80-year-old matron of his church. She guided him into her parlor to show him that classic painting of Daniel patting the head of the now-docile lions. "Notice, Brother Stanley, the reason Daniel was delivered was because he looked up at God, not down at the lions."

3. **Leaders repeat the fundamentals.**

When Vince Lombardi took over the fledgling Green Bay Packers decades ago, he gathered them into the locker room and held up the object of their attention. "Gentlemen, this is a football." Leaders begin with the fundamentals.

The text says that Asa commanded that the people follow God's commandments and that they enter into a covenant with the Lord.

It's fundamental: People want rules—People need rules—that are TUF:

T	ranscendent
U	niversal, and
F	irm.

TRANSCENDENT: They want rules that come from the highest moral source and not rules that are dependent upon the whims of politicians, dictators, or celebrities. They want to know that these rules or commandments are untarnished by any leader's desire for power or pleasure.

UNIVERSAL: People want to know that these rules apply to everyone, everywhere. These rules are not affected by sex, culture, or nationality. They apply to all people, everywhere.

FIRM: People want to know that these rules are firm. They do not bend to expediency, popularity, or prejudice.

Believe it or not, people want the Ten Commandments.

People recognize the necessity of rules. They recognize it with their pets. That's the reason they build fences in the backyard. They recognize it with street signs. People know they need rules for safe driving.

Increasingly, as Americans see their cities burning with chaos and feel their bellies burning with fear, they know (for reasons of personal and public security) they need rules that are TUF.

"God, give us leaders who will privately and publicly dramatize Your Ten Commandments, Your TUF rules, Lord."

4.   **Leaders obey God rather than man**.

Peter said it boldly.

"We must obey God rather than man." Jesus made it very specific. "He who loves his mother or father more than Me is not worthy of me." And Asa practiced it when he "threw Mama off the train." Asa deposed his mother Maacah from her queenly role.

I imagine mama screamed at this "disobedient son" the entire time.

5.   Leaders attract FAITHFUL followers.

The emphasis here is on <u>faith</u>. Leaders get people to follow either by force or by faith. Kings and dictators lead by force. Parents, teachers, and bosses often lead by force. Big mistake. The goal is to attract followers by faith, i.e. attracting people who <u>believe</u> in the leader's courage, vision, and integrity. People believe in the leader; therefore, they want to follow him or her.

No doubt there was an element of force in Asa's warriors following him into battle, but they could have defected, as many scared soldiers have done, but because of Asa's courage and faithfulness, the text says, "The people gladly followed him when they saw that the Lord his God was with him." (2 Chronicles 15:9)

6. **Leaders choose principle over profit or popularity.**

When Asa destroyed the temple shrines and Asherah idols, he was, in fact, destroying sorcery and sex-for-hire. That did not make him popular with the temple prostitutes or the fortune tellers.

I know a little bit about skirmishes on both these fronts.

We were in a restaurant inside a Boston mall. Two booths away, the restaurant had set up shop to have a money-making sorcery booth. While people waited for their food, the waitress came by with a card inviting them to go to that end booth to have their palms read, play tarot cards, and do Ouija. My wife and I watched in horror as the booth stayed busy with naïve people lining up to embrace the demonic. I felt the blood rise to the top of my ears as I walked to the booth, confronted the medium, and talked to the person having her palm read. "This is demonic. Don't do it."

I turned to the people in line and repeated it. "This is demonic. Don't do it."

I picked up my check and walked out of the restaurant. Halfway down the mall, I heard someone calling me, and I turned to see a raging bull.

"What are you doing, man? You're driving away business," screamed the restaurant manager.

"All I did, sir, was tell the truth. That's demonic activity back there. It will destroy their lives. It will destroy yours."

"You get out of here. Don't ever come back to this mall or this restaurant."

We did leave, and we never went back, but kept praying that the message penetrated somebody that day.

Another time, on a warm spring day, I was walking through Boston Common and saw a young man lying on a blanket, shirt open, sunning himself. I noticed two men in their late 20s, no shirts, in an open car cruising… stalking. They stopped the car, got out, and, holding hands, they started to walk toward the young man.

I said, "Hey, buddy, I don't know what you're waiting for, but if you're waiting for a homosexual pickup, you're about to get one."

His back shot up from the blanket. He rested on his two elbows, looked across the street, and saw the two guys heading for him. He said, "Thanks, mister." He buttoned his shirt, grabbed his blanket, and ran the other way.

I continued my walk, but not for long. The two predators cornered me near the fountain. "What did you tell that guy?"

"I told him he'd better leave."

I saw four fists clench in the corner of my eye, and I felt my knees melt like hot wax. I hyperventilated, catching short breaths, I felt acid spilling from my stomach, causing it to jerk and twist. "You know what I told him and why I told him, and if you want to slug me up for that, go ahead. God will still love you, and I'll still love you like God does, and besides, that's the same God that can change your lives."

I saw the fingers of their fists gradually unfurl. They turned to each other and walked away.

Like Jesus—and like Asa earlier—I saw the message repeated: **When you speak God's truth, they either love you or hate you.**

7. **Leaders pursue FAITHFULNESS rather than pursue rewards or recognition.**

Cynical observers of Mother Teresa's legendary compassion frequently whined: "There are still billions of people homeless and hungry and dying on the streets. What you're doing is just a do-good exercise and not really helping anyone."

Her reply was: "God has called me to a ministry of faithfulness, a ministry of service, not of success."

Asa's heart was with God, so he stepped forward in faithful service, not knowing the outcome and not looking for recognition.

8. **Leaders never know just how far-reaching their faithfulness extends.**

Ronald Reagan: "Mr. Gorbachev, tear down these walls." Reagan could not have anticipated the long-term effects of those words, which eventually freed 100-million people held hostage behind an iron curtain.

Asa certainly could not have anticipated that his divine heroism preserved the scarlet thread that eventually led to the blood-bought redemption of all mankind through Jesus Christ.

Leaders do not look for instant results. They obey, and they trust God for the results that will glorify Him and bring about His purposes.

9. **Godly leaders turn people back to God.**

After listening to Asa's prayer and watching his obedience in action, the people **gladly** followed the Lord. An entire nation returned to God.

Proverbs 29:2 NIV reminds us: "When the righteous thrive, the people rejoice; when the wicked rule, the people groan."

Under Asa, an entire nation returned to God.

"God, give us that kind of bold leadership for America."

10. **Finally, leaders are vulnerable. Leaders "never arrive."**

They must constantly turn back to God.

Later in life, after all those God-ordained victories and successes, Asa refused to listen to godly counsel. His life crumbled after that.

True leaders know: "When you're green, you're growing. When you're ripe, you're rotten."

Chapter 3

Why People Don't Claim Asa, and Why They Do

Three:

Why People Don't Claim Asa

> Help us, O God, for there is none like You
> to help the weak conquer the strong.
> We're here to meet this huge army
> because we trust in You and who You are.
> Don't let mere mortals stand against You.
>
> —2 Chronicles 14:11

Everyone faces huge armies. Screaming, crush-you-now armies.
Monster armies. Armies that:

    Melt your knees,

        Ignite cold sweat,

            Choke your throat,

                And stop your breathing.

Everyone faces these armies. So…

Why *wouldn't* a person want to claim Asa and enjoy the divine power it provides?

What person?

A Believer?

Or

A Non-believer?

By believers we mean Christians, those folks who believe in the power and the promises of the Bible.

By non-believers we mean atheists.

We do not mean "skeptics," "agnostics," or "doubters." There are no such entities as skeptics, agnostics, or doubters. Either you believe in God or you don't.

Your actions give you away.

Jesus dramatized this truth when he said, "No man can serve two masters. You either serve God or serve self." (Matthew 6:24)

If God is the master, you serve God and others. If self is the master, you serve yourself. Your actions betray your personal belief that there is no God. That's an atheist.

This truth about God has life-changing, world-changing, and eternity-changing consequences, because belief in God or non-belief in God applies to interactions with people. When we relate to people, our motive is to serve or to seduce.

Think this sounds extreme? Every time you have an interaction with someone, your goal is to help them. Or your goal is to get from them. Give or get. Is your goal to give, or is your goal to get?

It depends upon whether you're infused with the love or God, or whether you're infused with the love of power. The love of power is the same as saying that self is the master. Behavior betrays belief, and action dramatizes convictions. The only question is: Are your actions based upon justifiable, intelligent, loving, and reasonable beliefs?

Let's see.

Why Believers Don't Claim Asa:

- No knowledge
- Not worthy
- No courage
- No urgency
- No skill
- No time
- No obedience
- No faith
- No connection
- No patience

- **No Knowledge**

> "We didn't know!"

> "Hey... give us some slack. We just didn't know about this power."

> "Yuh, we read it, but we didn't know it was available today."

Great News: It's still available! The title is *The Prayer of Asa: God **Still** Loves To Do the Impossible through you.*

You heard the story of the guy who took a five-day Caribbean cruise. He boarded at Galveston and sailed to the usual ports around the Gulf of Mexico. Each evening, in his cabin, he unpacked his crackers, bananas, peanut butter, raisins, and bottles of orange juice. Upon his return, his friend greeted him to give him a ride back to Dallas. "How was the cruise?"

"Unbelievable. The quiet of the ocean was unbelievable. Sunrises and sunsets were glorious. It was very relaxing."

"Bet you had a fit over the food. Everyone does."

"Couldn't afford any of that. The buffets looked very appetizing, but I didn't bring enough money with me for that. I just brought my own snacks to eat."

"WHAT?! Didn't someone tell you the price of the ticket for the cruise includes all that food? You missed out on a five-day feast, buddy. Five days of 24/7 eating if you wanted it."

Our guy denied himself the pleasure of the food because **HE DID NOT KNOW**.

Christians deny themselves the pleasure and the power of Asa because they don't know that it's still available. They don't know those passages throughout the Bible that erupt with life and power like Old Faithful erupts with steamy columns of hot water.

> ...I no longer live, but Christ lives in me...

> —Galatians 2:20 NIV

God is in you to will and to work for his good purpose.

—Philippians 2:13 NIV

Christ in you, the hope of glory

—Colossians 1:27 NIV

In Christ we are more than conquerors.

—Romans 8:37 NIV

And on and on.

Not Worthy

Christians don't pray because of a faulty belief that they are not worthy. The attack goes something like this:

"I feel like a hypocrite praying. Especially praying for big things. I'm not Asa. I'm not Moses. I'm not the Apostle Paul. I'm not a Billy Graham or a C.S. Lewis. I'm not a minister or a priest, and I screw up in so many ways. I've done so many stupid and sinful things. I can't talk to God for anything, much less the big things. He probably wouldn't listen to me anyway."

Great News: We don't claim Asa because we are worthy. We claim Asa because God is.

And He's not just worthy, but willing to pour His power into us and through us.

It's like the cliché: "I can't go to church with all those good people. I'd be a hypocrite."

We go to church not because we are worthy, but because we need to. We go to church because we need to honor the one who made us. We go to church not because we're worthy, but because God is. We go to church because we need to encourage people in church, and we need their encouragement.

We pray to God, we go to church, not because of who we are, but because of Who He is.

Bill Hybels:

> I'm praying to the Creator of the world, the King of the universe, the all-powerful, all-knowing, all-faithful One. I'm praying to you, God, who made the mountains and who can move them if necessary. I'm praying to you, the One who has always been faithful to me, who has never let me down no matter how frightened I was or how difficult the situation looked. I'm praying to you, who wants to bear fruit through me, and I am going to trust that you

are going to use me tonight. Not because of who I am, but because of who you are. You are faithful![55]

—Bill Hybels

55 Bil Hybels, Lavonne Neff, and Ashley Wiersman, *Too Busy Not To Pray: Slowing Down to Be With God* (Downers Grover, IL: IVP Books, 2008) 79-81.

No Courage

"We fear the prayer of Asa because, well, we fear we might get an answer."

Praying Asa invites:
- Persecution
- Insult
- Introspection
- Misunderstanding
- Busting out of one's comfort zone.

We pray for love, and God plants us beside unloving people.

We pray for patience, and God sends trials.

We pray for submission, and God sends suffering.

We pray for unselfishness, and God sends uncomfortable opportunities to serve others.

We pray for strength, and we get tormented by Satan.

We pray to get closer to God, and we get attacked by friends who misunderstand us.

We get answers we didn't expect and get slammed with trials we didn't invite.

So… understandably… we don't pray big. We don't pray Asa, because God might answer those big prayers and send us big challenges.

Great News: We pray for victory and, yes, the world seems to sweep down upon us in a storm of temptation. But the promise is still there.

> This is the victory that has overcome the world, even our faith.
>
> —1 John 5:4 NIV

The victory that Asa claimed, the God that Asa served, is still here.

No Urgency

Dwight Moody emphasized that prayer must be a matter of urgency, because the disciples never asked Jesus, "Show us how to work, or show us how to preach, or show us how to teach." They asked, "Show us how to pray." And Jesus answered:

> 9Our Father which art in heaven, Hallowed be thy name.
>
> 10 Thy kingdom come, Thy will be done in earth, as it is in heaven.
>
> 11 Give us this day our daily bread.
>
> 12 And forgive us our debts, as we forgive our debtors.
>
> 13 And lead us not into temptation, but deliver us from evil: For thine is the kingdom, and the power, and the glory, for ever. Amen.
>
> —Matthew 6:9-13 KJV

Jesus' prayer is so urgent and so important, it can be summed as ACTS.

A Adoration

C Confession

T Thanksgiving

S Supplication

Say it now. Act on it now.

Great News: The power of the Asa prayer is in the Lord's Prayer.

No Skill

"I'm no theologian or preacher. I didn't even finish high
school. I don't know how to say any of those thees and
thous and whereases and wherefores. I'm not ready for
big prayer of Asa, because I don't know how to pray."

Great news: Folks think that prayer is like the majestic wording in the
Westminster Prayerbook:

"Merciful God, we confess we have sinned against Thee
in thought, word, and deed by what we have done and
left undone. We have not loved Thee with our whole
hearts. We have not loved our neighbors as ourselves.
We are truly sorry. We humbly repent. For the sake of
Your Son, Jesus Christ, have mercy on us and forgive us
that we may delight in Thy will and walk in Thy ways to
the glory of Thy name. Amen."

That's okay. You want to repeat out of a prayer book that expresses your
sincere desire? That's okay.

But it kinda' reminds me of the story of pilgrim John Smith. His mission was to deliver a message to Priscilla Alden. The message was an offer
of love from Miles Standish to Priscilla Alden. Upon reading it, Priscilla
looked at the messenger and said, "Speak for yourself, John."

Speak for yourself

Here's a simple prayer. You may not like it, but it's real:

"God, did you see what that guy just did? What a jerk.
He could have killed me. He could have killed both of
us. Pulling around on the right-hand side is illegal for
a reason, God. I feel like taking a gun, and like the old
gangster movies, reaching out my window and blowing
out his tires. God, thanks for the side-view mirror, that at

least I could see the guy coming at the last minute. Okay, I forgive him. Help him get where he wants to go safely. Thank you that my coffee didn't spill all over me when I had to make that quick cut. And yeah, that reminds me, the fact that I live in America where I have a car, where I can go wherever I want to anytime. Thank you, Lord, for the lessons from this near accident."

Great News: That's somebody talking to God expressing anger, hatred, forgiveness, and understanding. Real feelings. Praying, among other things, is reporting our feelings to God, talking honestly to God.

Dr. Charles Allen, the esteemed minister of First United Methodist Church in Houston, the nation's largest Methodist church, said that when people stopped praying, they started seeing psychiatrists in droves.

You don't need a lot of skill to enjoy the therapy and release of a gut-felt prayer. Just do it. Open your mouth and talk to the one who made you. He was there for Asa; He is here for you.

No Time

No time to claim Asa and ask God for daily victories? Too busy? Can't fit it in?

Great News: Start with your hand. Thumb is closest to you—reminds you to pray for those closest to you. Next, the index finger used for pointing—points to all the people you've ever had who have helped you. The third finger, the middle, is the tallest, and it reminds us to pray for our leaders. The fourth finger, the ring finger, is the weakest, as every pianist knows. It stands for those who are in trouble and pain and need the power of Asa. The little finger is the smallest and least important. It stands for yourself. Of course, you're looking at your whole hand, and the whole hand represents God, the God of Asa, who supports all fingers.

Billy Sunday gave a simple formula for the Christian life: 15, 15, and 15.

Let God talk to you 15 minutes a day (read your Bible), talk to God 15 minutes a day (prayer), and tell someone else about Christ 15 minutes a day (witness).

Decades ago, George Cohan wrote his memorable song, *Only 45 Minutes from Broadway:*[56]

Only forty-five minutes from Broadway
Think of the changes it brings
For the short time it takes
What a diff'rence it makes
In the ways of the people and things
Oh, what a fine bunch of rubens
Oh, what a gay atmosphere
They have whiskers like hay
And imagine Broadway
Only forty-five minutes from here

---

56 George M. Cohan, "Forty-Five Minutes from Broadway" from Broadway musical *Forty-Five Minutes from Broadway* (New York: F.A. Mills, 1906)

Only 45 minutes.

Don't have time? Pray while you're jogging, pray while you're cooking, pray while you're eating, pray while you're sitting, pray while you're standing, pray while you're lying down, pray while you're making love with your spouse, pray while you're walking to your car. Pray while you're in the restroom. Pray without ceasing. It's as normal as breathing. You've got time to breathe; you've got time to pray.

Only 45 minutes... What a difference it makes, and 15 of those minutes are praying.

Prayer is like breathing.

Inhale / exhale.

Inhale / exhale.

Inhale / exhale.

Inhale / exhale.

You've got time to breathe; you've got time to pray.

Suck in the big promises of Asa just like you sucked in the big gulps of air.

"I don't feel like praying. It doesn't make sense for God to command me to pray whenever I don't feel like it."

Great News: Prayer is a gift, isn't it? So if it's a gift, how can God command it?

Good question. The command to pray is a theme that runs throughout the Bible:

Paul said:

> [16]Be joyful always; [17]pray continually; [18]give thanks in all circumstances, for this is God's will for you in Christ Jesus.
>
> —1 Thessalonians 5:16-18

And he also said:

> I want men everywhere to lift up holy hands in prayer without anger or disputing.
>
> —1 Timothy 2:8 NIV

So why would God **command** prayer? What about the times we don't feel like doing it?

Tempted with the urge to surrender to sin, commit a crime, or collapse into suicide? That's exactly the time to lift your face out of the dirt of despair and expose yourself to the light of God's love and healing. That's prayer.

God commands us to pray because God knows this principle: Losers wait until they feel victorious before they act in a victorious way. Winners act in a victorious way, and the feeling of victory follows. And the starting line of their victorious action is prayer.

God commands us to pray because prayer, like the prayer of Asa, is therapeutic and effective and strengthens your bond with the Father who made us.

No Faith

> "What will be, will be. Prayer really doesn't change anything. Praying big, like praying the prayer of Asa, just gets your hopes up."

Great News: The prayer of a righteous man avails much, the Bible tells us. It's hard for us to accept that and act on it, because we live in a culture soaked in determinism, fatalism, chaos, sadism, humanism, and hedonism.

1. Determinism: There's nothing you can do to change anything. The universe is fixed. Your genes, your environment got you trapped.
2. Fatalism: It's ALL in God's hands. Don't even try. "Allah wills." (that type of mentality)
3. Chaos: There's no meaning and no purpose. We are evolutionary accidents.
4. Sadism: God is malicious and capricious. Prayer wouldn't move Him even if He was around.
5. Humanism: It's up to me. No deity will save me or help me. It's ALL up to me.
6. Hedonism: Pleasure is my kick. Who needs prayer?

The really great news is that smart and compassionate people keep praying, because they know that is the only way to prevent being ripped by the storms of life.

George Adam Smith tells the story about the time he was climbing the Weisshorn above the Zermatt Valley in Switzerland with two guides on a stormy day. They had made the ascent on the sheltered side. Reaching the top, and exhilarated by the thought of the view before him, Smith sprang to the top of the peak—and was almost blown away by the gale. The guide caught hold of him and pulled him down saying, "On your knees, sir! You are safe here only on your knees."

No Connection

"I don't see a connection between praying boldly for impossible tasks, expressed in Asa, and a simple prayer of cleansing my heart, expressed in the Beatitudes. One is asking for power and victory, and the other is asking for submission and service. How can it be the same God and the same Bible?"

Great News: Jesus Christ is the same yesterday, today, and forever. God's principles of power, victory, and service have flourished since the beginning of time and still apply today.

The Beatitudes and Asa:

> [3]"Blessed are the poor in spirit, for theirs is the kingdom of heaven.
>
> [4] Blessed are those who mourn, for they will be comforted.
>
> [5] Blessed are the meek, for they will inherit the earth.
>
> [6] Blessed are those who hunger and thirst for righteousness, for they will be filled.
>
> [7] Blessed are the merciful, for they will be shown mercy.
>
> [8] Blessed are the pure in heart, for they will see God.
>
> —Matthew 5:1-8 NIV

Beatitudes	The Prayer of Asa
1. Poor in Spirit	"Lord, there is none like you." An admission of our need for God.
2. Mourn, no pride	"The powerless against the mighty.
3. Meek used by God	"Help us, O Lord, for we rely upon You."
4. Hunger and thirst for righteousness to do God's will	"And in Your name we have come up against this vast army."
5. Pure in heart	"O Lord, You are our God." That's purity of heart. We do it for God and by God's power. That's the same as hunger and thirst for righteousness and being pure in heart.

No Patience

"I pray for power, and I pray and I pray, but nothing seems to work. It's useless."

Great News: It's like flying through a fog of clouds above Boston, or London, or San Francisco. When you're at 30,000 feet and look through the clouds, there it is: the dry, warm, clear sunshine.

It was always there. You just couldn't see it.

Talking about a plane... when I board, I first claim my version of Asa: "God, make my life a miracle of Your service today, so that You get the victories for whatever is won today."

Sometimes the prayer is answered right then. Sometimes it isn't.

This time I got an answer. Quick. I was in seat 6A on an American flight from New York to DFW, and I prayed that Asa prayer before boarding.

Had my Bible flopped open on my tray when the flight attendant came by to offer coffee.

"Can I talk to you about that later?" she said, pointing to the Bible.

Her name was Sammye, and I learned that she had been visiting the Highland Oaks church in Dallas and had a lot of questions. She returned with the coffee and sat in 6B and poured out a list of questions. I told her to come back after her duties were all done, so we'd have more time. Thirty minutes later, she returned, and I led her through John 3:16, Acts 2:38, Romans 10:7, and "the fruits of the spirit" from Galatians 5. I showed her how people acknowledged Christ in the first century, obeyed him, and became part of a fellowship of believers and subsequently lived a life of joy and service.

"That's what I want to do."

I led her to Christ right there in seats 6A and 6B. Her eagerness to learn and her questions were reminiscent of the Ethiopian official in Acts 8.

> [29] The Spirit told Philip, "Go to that chariot and stay near it."

³⁰ Then Philip ran up to the chariot and heard the man reading Isaiah the prophet. "Do you understand what you are reading?" Philip asked.

³¹ "How can I," he said, "unless someone explains it to me?" So he invited Philip to come up and sit with him.

³² This is the passage of Scripture the eunuch was reading:

"He was led like a sheep to the slaughter, and as a lamb before the shearer is silent, so he did not open his mouth.
³³ In his humiliation he was deprived of justice. Who can speak of his descendants? For his life was taken from the earth."

³⁴ The eunuch asked Philip, "Tell me, please, who is the prophet talking about, himself or someone else?" ³⁵ Then Philip began with that very passage of Scripture and told him the good news about Jesus.

³⁶ As they traveled along the road, they came to some water and the eunuch said, "Look, here is water. Why shouldn't I be baptized? ³⁸ And he gave orders to stop the chariot. Then both Philip and the eunuch went down into the water and Philip baptized him. ³⁹ When they came up out of the water, the Spirit of the Lord suddenly took Philip away, and the eunuch did not see him again, but went on his way rejoicing.

—Acts 8:29-39 NIV

I learned later that Sammye returned to the Highland Oaks church and visited with Gary Beauchamp, the preacher at that time who baptized her.

The impossible events throughout the Bible still occur today by people who patiently pray for them.

Why Non-believers Don't Claim Asa

Atheists don't claim Asa—atheists don't pray at all—because of four issues:

- Absurd
- Arrogant
- Anger
- Afraid

Absurd

    a.   Stupid

It is stupid to talk into the air. You may as well talk to tree. Talking to a tree actually would make more sense, because you know there's some kind of life in a tree. Sap is flowing in there, and branches are growing, but there's no sap and there's no growth in the tree. The only sap is the one mouthing words into the air.

The absurdity of prayer was characterized in a famous painting by Norman Rockwell called *Saying Grace*. It might as well have been called, "What's that crazy lady doing?" Because that's the expression on the face of the guys watching Grandma and her grandson praying.

Saying Grace, 1951

Prayer is so obviously absurd because you cannot know someone you cannot see. You cannot know someone you cannot hear.

Maybe.

For believers (and non-believers if they so choose), there is a way to know God through words, and those are the words in the book we call the Bible. The question is, can we really know someone by reading his or her words?

In an early novel, Pearl Buck told the story of a young soldier, Lester, in World War II. Lester was introduced by mail to Helen, who was back in the states. This is long before the days of emails, computers, cell phones, Facebook, and the rest.

Pen, paper, and postage stamps. That's it.

For years, they exchanged letters. They wrote their histories, passions, failures, desires, and plans.

Deeply. Intensely. So deep and so intense that they fell in love... by way of words on paper. Their first meeting was on their wedding day. War's over, Lester returns, hugs and kisses Helen at Grand Central Station, and from there they go to the altar to say their wedding vows.

Words...

They are pellets of passion to penetrate the hearts and minds of men and women.

Words... like the words in the Bible.

b. Counterproductive

Praying , according to the atheist, is not only absurd and stupid, but it's counterproductive. The pray-er is wrapped up in the empty exercise called prayer rather than in actions that produce the results that he or she wants. The pray-er is talking to the air rather than taking to the streets.

Prayer is not only absurd, but it's a crutch, an escape, an opium for the masses, as Karl Marx said.

Prayer, and the act of praying, blind us from the realities of life as the humanists (atheists) express it in their Humanist Manifesto.

- Knowledge of the world is derived by observation, experimentation, and rational analysis.
- Humans are an integral part of nature, the result of unguided <u>evolutionary</u> change.
- <u>Ethical</u> values are derived from human need and interest as tested by experience.
- Life's fulfillment emerges from individual participation in the service of humane ideals.
- Humans are social by nature and find meaning in relationships.
- Working to benefit society maximizes individual happiness.

Nice theory.

But where are the orphanages, homeless havens, rescue shelters, and mission hospitals built by these self-deceived atheists who refuse to pray?

Answer: There aren't any.

c.   Dangerous

People use prayer to justify:

- God told me to steal the car.
- God told me to leave my family.
- God (Allah) told me to ram into the Twin Towers.
- God told me it was okay to use heroin. Hey, it makes me feel so good.
- God told me, told me, told me. God showed me, showed me, showed me.

True, petitions to God are often abused, but abuse doesn't mean that the thing itself is wrong. A sharp pencil can be used to stab someone. It doesn't mean the pencil is bad. A car can be used to smash into a bus full of school children. It doesn't mean that the car itself is bad.

Atheists recoil from prayer because they "know" that Christians (allegedly) use it as a dangerous activity to justify anything. What the atheist doesn't know is that the real God—the God of the Bible—never asks people to do anything that violates His word, or that violates human life or dignity.

God's words are expressed in the Bible, which is an objective, loving source, a set of rules designed to help people.

"God told me to ram into the Twin Towers!"

(You're listening to the wrong God.)

"God told me to lay all my paycheck on the lottery!"

(You're listening to the wrong God.)

"God told me to leave my wife and family!"

(You're listening to the wrong God.)

The Bible warned us about that type of deceit. There is a force called Satan, who presents himself sometimes as an angel of light, and in a moment of passion can appear to sound like the voice of God.

Arrogance

"No one's going to tell me what to do. I need no authority outside of me. I commit "sin" (to use that word popular with Christians) only when I do things I do not want to do, or when I express beliefs which are not mine."

I know about authority.

I know what it feels like to resent it. I know the humiliation one feels when you have to recognize it and obey it.

Authority: Respect it, you win. Curse it, you lose.

4:15 in the morning. Driving to the gym. Run, lift, and swim. Early. Beat the crowd.

Be at my desk by 6:00. Quiet. Bible study. Writing. Review schedule. A good day ahead.

…but not this one.

Driving slow. No dangers. No traffic. Cop stops me.

He hits me in the eye with a flashlight blazing as hot as a torch. "License and registration, please." Bald, bad, and big. A Hulk Hogan.

I shove my fingers into the glove compartment, hardly aware that I'm awake. My fingers slide over half-empty Chapstick bottles. My right index finger rams into a toothpick. I feel hills of wrapped peppermints underneath my palm. The insurance card. Got it. I reach into the seat pocket for my billfold and license.

With one hand, I slide license and insurance card into his palm. With the other, I hold my palm up to shield my eyes from the blinding light.

"Do you know what I stopped you for?"

"No, sir."

"You didn't put on your turn signal."

WHAAAT? I screamed in my skull. *It's 4:30 in the freaking morning. There's no one around for miles.*

He stomps to his car and calls the dispatcher to see if I'm a serial murderer.

Marches back. "Thank you, sir. Everything's fine. You can go, By the way, it doesn't matter if it's early in the morning or late at night or two in the afternoon. You've got to obey the laws and put on your directional when you turn."

I feel blood bubbling and rising in my jawbone. I want to say, *Haven't you got something better to do? Why aren't you out chasing the real crooks? Why aren't you driving up and down the alleys looking for hookers? Why aren't you on the freeway stopping speedsters?* But I didn't say anything. Instead, I said, "Yes sir. Thanks for stopping me, sir."

And he says, "I'm just going to give you a warning now. Have a great day and a great workout."

My blood cools down as I return the license and insurance to the glove compartment and seat pocket.

Authority. Respect it and move forward. Loathe it and you get whacked.

Tell me, what would have happened if I'd said, "I'll turn on the directional only when I want to, only when there are cars around. You have no authority to tell me when to turn on my directional. It's stupid for me to obey rules about turning on a directional when there's nobody around."

Yes, you're right. If the cop had been in a bad mood, he could have even hauled me in on trumped up charges. At the very least, I would have gotten a ticket and been forced to pay what, fifty bucks, a hundred bucks?

Authority. Love it and you move forward. Loathe it and you're moving backward.

It's the story of the puppy in the yard. You have a fence around the yard. The fence represents rules and authority. The puppy stays inside the fence, and he's safe. He can play and romp. Outside of the fence, the truck smashes him. The owner of the puppy builds a fence because he loves the puppy.

Anger

The atheist is mad at God for a general reason and a specific reason.

GENERAL:

If there were a God, He would stop pain. For everybody. Everywhere.
- No Holocaust
- No famine
- No tsunamis
- No rape
- No wife beatings
- No cancer

SPECIFIC:

"How could you? (Yeah, God, I'm talking to you.)

"How could you let:
- My wife betray me, run off with a young guy, and leave me with all these kids?"
- My son get killed by that drunk driver roaring down I-40 on the wrong side?"
- My father die of a heart attack and plunge us into poverty?"
- My boss seduce me and then threaten to fire me if I said anything?"

"How could you? How could you let this happen?"

Some people who say this are atheists who used to be Christians. They trashed the Christian perspective because of tragedies like the above.

They collapsed into Pascal's dilemma.
- The Bible teaches that God is all powerful and all loving. Either God is too weak to stop pain, in which case God has no power.

- God doesn't care, in which case He has no love.

Either way, people reject Him because, well, there's nothing to reject. He doesn't exist.

No power and no love equals no God.

I know a little bit about pain and its relation to God.

I slammed my forehead on the tile floor demanding, begging, pleading, ordering God to stop the pain stabbing me at the upper spine, at the back of my neck. I don't want another Hydrocodone or Valium. They make me so depressed, even suicidal.

"God, stop that sharp, hot pain. Stop it. Put Your hand on it like Jesus did with the blind man on his eyes. And why did you let that guy slam into me years ago in that rear-end collision? Crushed the car, snapped my neck, and now I have a lifetime of pain. And why, O God, and why, why, why…"

And why the childhood of despair, hunger, and poverty? And why that "acid-in-your-face" scarring my mother and driving her to suicide?

I gave sketchy details earlier. Here's "the rest of the story."

I don't know why he was sick all the time. No one else's father was. He was always either coughing, wheezing, choking, in comas, and in and out of hospitals. When would he get well? When would we be a "normal" family? I guess never.

His TB put us on welfare, taking him from his back-breaking job in that damp, dirty mill. It landed him in that infamous Boston sanatorium, miles down the road from our tenement in Lawrence—the "armpit of the east"—memorialized in Alan Farnham's book and described earlier in this book:

There were no 'Café Budapests' in Lawrence… the section where mills were located was considered by locals to be among the city's toughest- a wasteland of shuttered shops and broken windows…

Life for working men and women in Lawrence had never been easy (the city was the scene for the 1912's Bread and Roses strike by 25,000 workers), but at least the city had once bustled with commercial activity. Now, it ranked twenty-fourth among the poorest cities in the United States, no longer famous for manufacturing, but for being a crack-cocaine capital and a magnet for newly-arrived immigrants. Though only 30 miles north of Boston, it might as well have been in the third world.[57]

And, in our patch of the "third world" (our tenement of broken windows crushed between shuttered shops, across from the mills), things never got better, only worse… and only to us. That's how it looked to a hungry thirteen-year-old, clothed in Salvation Army discards, crouched in an icy corner room in December.

Suicide.

Why not? At least I wouldn't have to look at those guys anymore: Charlie Grady, Eddie Wacker or Lennie Gaboury. They lived in matchbox tenements like we did; but the rest was different.

They had cars. They had refrigerators. They had heat in the winter. They had paychecks coming in each week.

They never had their lights and heat shut off. They never were evicted in the chill of winter. They never were denied food. (As many times as it happens, you never get used to having a glass of water for breakfast … and lunch … and supper.)

---

57 See, Forbes: Great Success Stories, by Alan Farnham, © 2000, Forbes. Inc., published by John Wiley and Sons. P.4

They didn't hear dishes—pitched at a drunken father—smash against kitchen walls. They didn't hear a mother wail and scream, watching beer destroy a sick man whose lust for beer kept food from the mouths of two sons.

And Grady and Wacker and Gaboury were never blasted out of bed by a pale mother wailing, "He's gone again. Come in here!" And we did.

Because of his drinking, poor eating, and failing to take adequate insulin, he—a diabetic—slipped again into a coma. Morning after morning, we poured orange juice and sugared water down his gurgling, resisting throat.

Why do I have to be the only kid in school who can't bring friends home? Why do I have to be the only kid without a dime to buy a waxed cup of ice cream in the cafeteria? Why do I have to be the only kid who can never buy one of those vanilla cokes on the way home?

Why can't we ever buy fresh milk? Why do we always have to drink that yellow, lumpy, powdery stuff in dust-brown bags that welfare gives us? And why do my brother and I have to be the only kids in the Boy Scout troop wearing patched street-clothes instead of crisp uniforms?

Because welfare doesn't give money for an ice cream, a Coke, fresh milk, or a boy scout uniform.

This dragged on for years.

When I was fifteen, I watched him die in my mother's lap. She was sitting and he was propped up across her lap. Frantically, she rubbed her hands up and down his back; back and forth across his caved-in chest, trying to revive him. His mustard-yellow face fell back; his cold, damp body hung across her arms. Propping him up again, she rained tears on his motionless body, looking like Pietà Mary, in agony over a limp, cold form.

He died quickly. Her fierce loyalty kept him alive for many years. Now, it was over. He was dead.

It was mid-January. A puke-smelling, freezer-box, third-floor welfare tenement was the stage of death.

His death occurred during a rare happy moment in their lives. Following three months of separation, they decided to try it again. They were determined to stop screaming and cursing. They were determined to love ... again.

He was not going to drink. He was going to take his medicine regularly.

They were reunited only a few weeks—no drunken fights, no comas. He really took care of himself. That Sunday afternoon, they took a quick nap. His self-injected insulin shot wasn't due for a couple of hours ... no problem.

But they overslept. She woke up and found him swooning off in a coma. Orange juice. Sugared water. He coughed, gurgled and swallowed. Looked routine. We waited ... no response. More orange juice, more sugared water. It wouldn't go down. It filled and overflowed his open mouth, like racing tap water overflowing a glass. Streams of orange spilled over his blue-gray lips, cascading down his salt-and-pepper stubbled chin. Too late. The doctor later said his heart simply could stand no more comas.

Others dictated funeral and burial arrangements. (Welfare's lousy for handling death.) We had no choice. We had no money and no insurance. I didn't understand it.

Mother went back to work for $40 a week and we still couldn't afford our holes-in-the-wall, and rats-in-the-closet tenement. I didn't have time for complaining or shaking my fist at God. I worked full-time and finished high school and turned the check over to my mother. When I finished high school, I continued to work full-time and attended college at her urging. I worked fifty hours a week, and earned that degree during the day, becoming the first one in my family to do so.

I channeled my experience with pain and suffering into joining the Peace Corps and transferring my energy into serving the worst, lepers in leper colonies in northwest Thailand.

I don't know why all that pain and tragedy happened to me, but I do know the pain is real and we have a choice.

Pain: what is.

Suffering: what I wish it could be.

When we accept the reality of pain (pain is), we can turn pain into progress. When we scream about the unfairness of suffering, we cripple ourselves, block our recovery, and hinder our efforts to serve others. It's a choice.

Fifty years ago. Charles Templeton was the preaching colleague of Billy Graham. They started the Billy Graham Evangelistic Association together. Charles Templeton decided he couldn't stomach preaching about the love of God anymore. He saw a picture on the cover of Life Magazine of a woman holding an infant thirsting to death in the middle of the Sudan, and he said, "Why couldn't God brinig just one cup of water with all His power and love? What would have been so difficult about that? Therefore, there is no God."

What I want to say to Charles Templeton is, "Charles, get off your butt and you go over there and do it."

In Northern England, there's a small village which still boasts a statue of Christ in the middle of the village. That statue and that town, was bombed during World War II. When they rebuilt it, they restored the statue of Christ and hoisted it in the middle of the square again. Instead of cementing the hands back on, the village leaders suggested leaving the hands off, with a plaque underneath: "Christ has no hands but ours."

When you turn cursing and complaining inward, you rapidly learn this truth:

> That which we complain about,
> we get more of.

Turn cursing and complaining inward, and it metastasizes like a cancer. But that energy of anger turned outward into service erupts into magnificent service to others and therapy for yourself.

The flip side of the coin of this truth about complaining is the following:

> That which we give gratitude for, we
> get more of.

Turning gratitude and praise outward, and it magnifies and expands like yeast inside rising dough.

Bottom line: Anger against God for the pain in the world is just flat ignorance.

Pain IS. It's real. So what do we do about it?

We take that anger, which is simply pent up energy, and convert it into service.

That's how smart and compassionate people diffuse their anger and direct it in productive ways.

We don't waste time or energy complaining or cursing. We act, with compassion, to stop or relieve the pain in the world. We realize we can't do everything, but we can do something.

<u>Afraid</u>

"What if I pray and find out there really IS a God? Would He or She, whatever care about me, help me? Let's go with He. Is He capricious, malicious, and arbitrary? What if there really is a Heaven? What if there really is a Hell? I've got some tough, tough decisions to make."

The atheist fears:

1. Introspection

The thoroughly committed atheist doesn't see anything wrong with his evil nature. "Leave me alone." He doesn't want to change anything. But, as esteemed atheist turning Christian, C.S. Lewis observed (from his own experience), when the atheist comes closer and closer to becoming a Christian, he looks back and sees how deceived he was. It's a gradual and frightening revelation. To eschew this revelation, the atheist dare not engage in introspection.

2. Acceptance

"I'm all I've got. This is who I am. And, God, You may not like me if I accept You as the God of the Bible."

For the word of God is living and active. Sharper than any double-edged sword, it penetrates even to dividing soul and spirit, joints and marrow; it judges the thoughts and attitudes of the heart.
—Hebrews 4:12 NIV

It's true:

It's embarrassing, humiliating, and scary to realize the core of the evil nature lurking in man. As Jeremiah said, "The human heart is desperately wicked. Who could understand it?"

The good, good, good news is that God knows that, and that's why, in the person of Jesus, He went to the cross. He knows all about our evil nature, and that's why He runs to embrace us and accept us just as we are. Just like He showered His love and acceptance on the woman caught in adultery in John 8.

3. Commission

"God, if I acknowledge Your presence and Your loving authority in my life, You may call me to a task that I do not want. That's scary."

Here, the atheist does not understand this liberating principle: God does not look at our ability or inability. He looks at our availability and provides the resources. When he sends us on a mission, he sends the manpower and materials to accomplish the mission, even though we can't see the manpower and materials ahead of time.

4. Rejection

"I'll lose my friends. They're all atheists, and our conversation is always about what hypocrites Christians are and how stupid belief in God is. I will be one of those that we mocked. I'll be an object of scorn."

I know what that feels like. My Ivy League buddies said of me, "Gallagher's gone off the deep end."

Then I realized that the deep end is for those:

- who have no guardrails,

- who have no grip on the steering wheel, and

- who don't know where they're going.

Those are the people who roll into a ditch and into destruction.

And, may I say, my atheist friend:

- I commend you for being so open-minded that you have read this far in the book.

- No need for you to roll into a ditch of destruction.

- There is a God of Love who loves you and will reveal Himself to you. He makes Himself known to those "who earnestly seek him," the Bible says.

- Then, you will need not be afraid, for "Perfect love casts out fear."

Epilogue

Asa Today

Okay, we've come full circle. Centuries ago, Asa appealed to a powerful God for an impossible military victory.

Three events in modern military history dramatize the power and relevance of that appeal today.

And in the face of impossible odds.

World War II: The Great Raid.

The scene: One hundred twenty Army Rangers crouched on the outskirts of Cabanatuan ready to rescue five hundred POWs, the remnants of the infamous Bataan death march.

Now, after three years of torture, slave labor, and one-cup-of-rice-a-day diets, these five hundred were walking skeletons convinced that their country had forgotten them.

Their country, and its military, in the person of one hundred twenty Rangers, was about to show them, "We haven't forgotten, and we're here to rescue," a rescue that would later be called the most daring rescue mission of our time, or The Great Raid.

It was "great" not merely because of the heroic victory, but because of the impossible odds.

One hundred twenty Rangers vs. two hundred Japanese troops inside Cabanatuan.

Nearly two-to-one odds.

(Sound familiar?)

Gets worse.

A mile away, well fortified in the lush Philippine jungle, was a contingent of one thousand Japanese troops ready to roar into action if trouble erupted at Cabanatuan.

The Great Raid had to be swift, total, and overpowering.

The Great Raid needed a miracle.

(Sound familiar?)

So… on the morning before the launch, Captain Mucci gathered his men. "Our buddies are in there, and they've been through Hell. We're about to go into that Hell. You're hard, and tough, and well trained, but we face impossible odds. We need courage and guts and determination that goes beyond what any of us can deliver. Get down on your knees now, every one of you, and pray like you've never prayed before. We need divine victory, and we don't need any damned atheists on this mission."

And they prayed.

They prayed and attacked and won.

The rest is history. The impossible triumphed, and you can see it on the movie, *The Great Raid*.

World War II: Iwo Jima

Iwo Jima: "The most savage and costly battle in the history of the Marine Corps." (General Holland).

The first wave of Marines to hit the beach numbered 230. By the end of the day, from this first wave, there were 185 dead bodies on the beach.

This first day's carnage presaged what as to happen over the next "36 days of Hell," as one reporter put it. Before the Iwo Jima battle was over, 6,829 Marines would be killed and 22,000 wounded.

The capture of Iwo Jima (Japan's strategic island/airfield) was essential to the Allies' war effort in defeating Japan and gaining control of the Pacific.

"Without this critical victory," as another reporter put it, "we would all be Japanese POWs today."

The battle was fierce and bloody.

Unknown to the Marines, 23,000 Japanese soldiers, trained in Samurai ferocity and drilled to "fight until death" were hidden in caves and tunnels throughout the island. They could see the approaching enemy (the

Marines), but the enemy could not see them. It was "the most ingenuous fortress the world had ever seen."

Despite the heavy casualties and seemingly impossible odds, the Marines prevailed, and the first trophy in victory was Mount Suribachi, the tall and distinct mountain dominating the island from the southern tip.

On the day before, while still onboard their troop ships, the Marines were led by their Catholic, Protestant, and Jewish chaplains praying for victory.

On the night before, General Smith spent the evening reading his Bible and praying all night... praying for a victory against impossible odds.

And victory they got.

After three days of bloody fighting, the Marines seized Mount Suribachi and erected the now-famous flag you see pictured here.

And they held an Easter service on the Mount.

CALL TO WORSHIP

INVOCATION

LORD'S PRAYER

HYMN (by audience):
> All hail the power of Jesus' name! Let angels prostrate fall;
> Bring forth the royal diadem, And crown Him Lord of all,
> Bring forth the royal diadem, And crown Him Lord of all.
>
> Let every kindred, every tribe, On this terrestrial ball,
> To Him all majesty ascribe, And crown Him Lord of all,
> To Him all majesty ascribe, And crown Him Lord of all.
>
> O that with yonder sacred throng, We at His feet may fall;
> We'll join the everlasting song, And crown Him Lord of all,
> We'll join the everlasting song, And crown Him Lord of all.

RESPONSIVE READING--23rd Psalm:
> The Lord is my Shepherd; I shall not want.
> He maketh me to lie down in green pastures. He leadeth
> me beside the still waters.
> He restoreth my soul: He leadeth me in the paths of
> righteousness for His name's sake.
> Yea, though I walk through the valley of the shadow
> of death, I will fear no evil: for Thou art with me; Thy
> rod and Thy staff they comfort me.
> Thou preparest a table before me in the presence of
> mine enemies; Thou anointest my head with oil; my cup
> runneth over.
> Surely goodness and mercy shall follow me all the days
> of my life: and I will dwell in the House of the Lord forever.

SPECIAL MUSIC (Quartet)

SCRIPTURE--(Mark 16, 1-8)

PRAYER

SPECIAL MUSIC (Solo)

EASTER MESSAGE

HYMN (by audience):
> Love divine, all loves excelling, Joy of heaven, to earth
> come down;
> Fix in us Thy humble dwelling, All Thy faithful mercies crown.
> Jesus, Thou art all compassion, Pure, unbounded love Thou art;
> Visit us with Thy salvation, Enter every trembling heart.
>
> Breathe, O breathe Thy loving Spirit Into every troubled breast!
> Let us all in Thee inherit; Let us find the promised rest;
> Take away the love of sinning; Alpha and Omega be;
> End of faith, as its beginning, Set our hearts at liberty.
>
> Finish, then, Thy new creation; Pure and spotless let us be;
> Let us see Thy great salvation Perfectly restored in Thee;
> Changed from glory into glory Till in heaven we take our place,
> Till we cast our crowns before Thee, Lost in wonder, love,
> and praise.

BENEDICTION

CLOSING PRAYER (sung by audience)
> Our father's God, to thee, Author of liberty,
> To thee we sing; Long may our land be bright With freedom's
> holy light;
> Protect us by thy might, Great God, our King. Amen.

I realize this copy is splotchy and disjointed, but it's the original worship service that was banged out on a portable typewriter on Mount Suribachi.

The Marines didn't seize Suribachi for the purposes of applauding atheism or surrendering to political correctness. They didn't ask anyone's permission whether it would violate "separation of church and state" (a legal fiction). They honored the God and the biblical principles which are the foundation of this country and were the ultimate foundation of the American military forces.

The divine victory was accomplished against impossible odds.

Korean War: The Chosin Few

The scene: Twelve thousand American troops facing 120,000 Chinese troops in minus 30° weather at the Chosin Reservoir, Korea.

MINUS 30° weather: a chilling, killing temp.

"We are surrounded," announced the commander, "so we can attack and advance in any direction."

That was the legendary charge to the 12,000 freezing Marines. They were about to enter a battle later historians would call "The Iwo Jima of the Korean war."

Their mission: "Stop Chinese and North Korean troops from overrunning South Korea," were the orders from the top. General Douglas MacArthur.

But, to advance, these Marines needed a bridge. Air Support was sending one. The problem was: ground troops could see nothing in the sky, and the supply plane could see nothing on ground. Cloud cover was dense and low, touching the earth.

Here's how Marine General William Clary remembers the story: "We prayed, and prayed, and prayed to God for the heavens to open. From a pure weather standpoint, it was impossible.

"But the clouds parted that night, and we saw one big, glowing star. That star, by the way, has become the symbol of the Chosin Few Memorial.

"Daybreak saw the further dissipation of clouds and the appearance of supply planes to drop the food, medical supplies, and badly needed parts needed for the bridge. The problem then was that those 120,000 Chinese troops were bearing down on 12,000 Marines, blocking our efforts to build the bridge and to continue our advance."

"We prayed, and prayed, and prayed again against these impossible odds," said General Clary. "We built the bridge and we repelled the Chinese, an impossible task. We called it a divine victory. If God hadn't been with us, we just would not have made it."

They did make it, and there is now a memorial to the Chosin Few:

The base of the memorial says, "For you, the Chosin Few, the Eternal Band of Brothers."

Commenting on the Chosin Few Memorial, Colonel Paul Torres said, "The courage shown by the Marines at the Chosin Reservoir was an example of their resolve to fight against what seemed like impossible odds."